Promoting READING in Developing Countries

VINCENT GREANEY

World Bank, Washington, DC

Editor

INTERNATIONAL READING ASSOCIATION
800 Barksdale Road, PO Box 8139
Newark, Delaware 19714-8139, USA

The International Reading Association attempts, through its publications, to provide a forum for a wide spectrum of opinions on reading. This policy permits divergent viewpoints without implying the endorsement of the Association.

Director of Publications   Joan M. Irwin
Assistant Director of Publications   Wendy Lapham Russ
Senior Editor   Christian A. Kempers
Associate Editor   Matthew W. Baker
Assistant Editor   Janet S. Parrack
Editorial Assistant   Cynthia C. Sawaya
Production Department Manager   Iona Sauscermen
Graphic Design Coordinator   Boni Nash
Design Consultant   Larry F. Husfelt
Desktop Publishing Supervisor   Wendy A. Mazur
Desktop Publisher   Anette Schütz-Ruff
Desktop Publisher   Cheryl J. Strum
Production Services Editor   David K. Roberts

Cover Photograph: A daycare facility in Bangladesh provides an early education. Copyright by the World Bank. Used by permission.

Library of Congress Cataloging-in-Publication Data
   Promoting reading in developing countries/Vincent Greaney, editor.
      p.   cm.
   Includes bibliographical references and index.
      1. Literacy—Developing countries.   2. Literacy programs—Developing countries.
3. Books and reading—Developing countries.   4. Publishers and publishing—
Developing countries.   I. Greaney, Vincent.   II. International Reading Association.
LC161.P76   1996   96-22713
302.2'244'091724—dc20
ISBN 0-87207-239-8 (pbk.)

Dedication

TO THE MILLIONS of teachers throughout the developing world who, in spite of terrific odds, attempt to introduce young children to the power and magic of the printed word. In this way they open the possibility of a better world for their students and for future generations.

Contents

Foreword

SOME YEARS AGO I walked down 16th Street in Washington, DC, with a successful literacy worker from the Organization of American States. As we chatted, he said, "In the country I just left, we have many new literates, but they have nothing to read. What can we do to get materials into their hands?"

Literacy workers throughout the world still face this same dilemma today: how to provide access to quality reading materials to those who most need them, in situations where resources for education are the most difficult to acquire. *Promoting Reading in Developing Countries* offers some solid ideas about how this dilemma can be approached in creative ways. Each of the contributors to this book has dealt personally with the important problem of providing materials for readers, and each is knowledgeable about both the research background and the various ingenious and effective approaches to book publishing, printing, and distribution in developing countries.

In Chapter 1, Vincent Greaney discusses problems and issues related to reading and literacy promotion in the developing world. This chapter sets the tone for other important topics that are presented by the many distinguished contributors to this volume. These topics encompass the specific ways countries can increase literacy levels, and they explore the larger issues of how literacy acquisition and adequate access, distribution, and localized publishing efforts affect the social and economic growth of individuals, communities, and societies.

Some of the approaches undertaken in this volume are more comprehensive than others, but all offer possible solutions to a difficult challenge. Although many perspectives are presented, no single approach seems to be the final answer to the problem of providing access to reading materials. Variations in a country's economic and cultural conditions are major influences in literacy and publishing activities. The contributions made by the researchers, scholars, and literacy educators whose work appears in *Promoting Reading in Developing Countries* provide new directions for those working at all levels in the fascinating and challenging field of promoting reading in all countries of the world.

If I met my colleague from the Organization of American States today, I am sure that he would still be asking how he could get materials into the hands of the newly literate. This is a challenge that will take an enormous effort to overcome. However, as this book proves, the literacy community is finding solutions to this daunting problem. One hopes that with the publication of *Promoting Reading in Developing Countries*, these solutions may be shared by many.

Ralph C. Staiger
Emeritus Executive Director, International Reading Association

Acknowledgments

A DEEP DEBT of gratitude is owed to the contributors to the various chapters in this volume. Thanks are also due to Jim Socknat, who provided the necessary support and encouragement; to Sakhevar Diop and Betty Jane Greaney for comments on individual chapters; to Julie-Anne Graitge, Masako Nishio, Mako Takahashi Welch, and Lorena Wilmot for their assistance in preparing the manuscript; and to Joan Irwin, International Reading Association Director of Publications, who commissioned the book. A very special word of appreciation to Chris Kempers whose professionalism greatly enhanced the final product.

Contributors

Richard C. Anderson
Professor and Director, Center for the Study of Reading, University of Illinois, Champaign, Illinois, USA

Suzanne M. Deehy
Project Director, Sabre Foundation, Inc., Cambridge, Massachusetts, USA

Brigitte Duces
Senior Operations Officer, World Bank, Washington, DC, USA

Rosamaria Durand
Program Specialist, Book and Copyright Division, United Nations Educational, Scientific and Cultural Organization, Paris, France

Warwick B. Elley
Emeritus Professor of Education, University of Canterbury, Canterbury, New Zealand

Vincent Greaney
Senior Education Specialist, World Bank, Washington, DC, USA

Rebecca Knuth
Assistant Professor, School of Library and Information Studies, University of Hawaii, Honolulu, Hawaii, USA

João Oliveira
President, JM Associates, Brasília, Brazil

Barbara Perry
Chief Librarian, Joint World Bank–International Monetary Fund Library, Washington, DC, USA

Tony Read
Managing Director, International Book Development, London, England

Nelson Rodríguez-Trujillo
Managing Director, Psico Consult C.A., Caracas, Venezuela

Scott Walter
Director of International Development, International Reading Association, Newark, Delaware, USA

Introduction

ONE OF THE most important steps a country can take to improve its economy and increase personal growth opportunities for its people is to provide quality education to all. Arguably, the most important element of a quality education program is literacy. Without the ability to read, people are denied access to pertinent information about health, social, cultural, and political issues as well as sources of pleasure and enrichment.

For a population to become literate, it must have access to a supply of relevant and enlivening textbooks and supplementary reading material. Young people especially need access to high-quality books to develop not only the ability to read but also the reading habit. In most developed countries, a sophisticated book publishing industry makes it possible for people to access high-quality books and other reading materials. However, most countries located in developing areas of the world struggle in their indigenous publishing efforts. These countries, which are involved in the extremely complex tasks of nation building, have urgent requirements for print materials. And, as argued by the authors of this volume, developing countries require books printed in local languages that reflect local customs and cultures; these countries should not be dependent on imported books that have been published abroad.

1

In this book the authors provide valuable insights into the issues involved with literacy promotion in the developing countries of Africa, Asia, and South America. They present the unique challenges faced by countries with few resources for providing education and supporting publishing efforts, and they offer some suggestions and solutions for increasing the developing world's access to quality indigenous reading materials.

Almost all the authors in this volume have considerable practical experience in attempting to improve literacy levels in developing countries. The range of experience includes developing publishing capacity, introducing new reading methodologies, teaching, developing World Bank educational projects, conducting research and evaluation, conducting cross-cultural studies, supplying donated books, and supporting library development. This work has been conducted in South and East Asia, Africa, Latin America, Eastern Europe, and the Pacific Region.

Most of the topics covered in this book originally were presented at a World Bank–sponsored seminar in December 1992. Subsequently these presentations were substantially rewritten and made current. Additional contributions were invited, and an introductory overview chapter was added.

In ten chapters, the authors address the major issues involved in determining why global literacy is important and how to achieve this goal. In Chapter 1, I provide data on literacy achievement in developing countries and offer reasons why young people have not learned to read. Basic problems associated with the provision of textbooks and supplementary reading material are discussed. I then offer recommendations for improving literacy rates in developing countries.

In Chapter 2, Warwick Elley presents achievement results for the developing countries that participated in the International Association for the Evaluation of Educational Achievement Study of Reading Literacy. Elley explains the teaching and programmatic implications of this study, and he concludes that more books and literature-based instruction are needed to raise literacy levels in developing countries.

In the next chapter, Richard Anderson reviews the research literature that supports the many suppositions in this volume that argue that the most important way for teachers to promote active reading and vocabulary growth is to encourage wide reading. Student motivation, access to books, and teaching methodology are identified as key factors in the promotion of the reading habit.

João Oliveira, in Chapter 4, emphasizes the significance of using textbooks in developing countries. Although Oliveira agrees with the other authors in this volume that supplementary reading materials often greatly benefit the reading skills and attitudes of children in developing countries, he argues that textbooks, despite their drawbacks, will continue to be a major feature in curriculum delivery. He offers suggestions for ways textbooks can be improved by using some features of supplementary reading materials.

Tony Read outlines the problems associated with local publishing in developing countries in Chapter 5. Read contends that without a market, local publishing capacity cannot be sustained. Factors contributing to the lack of a viable publishing market include the low level of parental, school, and library demand; inadequate distribution systems; and the absence of a regional market for locally produced books. Lack of resources also results in low production levels of books. Read offers specific guidelines for improving local publishing capacity.

In the next chapter, Nelson Rodríguez-Trujillo discusses specific independent reading programs in Venezuela and Colombia. Evaluations of these programs focus on their impact on reading achievement and highlight the importance of teacher training, the need for access to a wide variety of reading materials, and the need for strong financial and administrative support.

Africa's "book famine" is attributed to the monopolization of the textbook market by government bodies, which has contributed to the demise of local publishers. In Chapter 7, Scott Walter gives an overview of several successful publishing efforts in African countries and discusses proposals for supporting indigenous publishing in Africa, including subsidizing purchasing power rather than production, enlarging the book trade, and creating an environment that supports new publishers.

In Chapter 8, Warwick Elley outlines the rationale for the book flood approach and procedures for establishing book floods. He also offers empirical evidence on the effectiveness of book floods derived from studies conducted in Fiji, Singapore, Niue, and the United Kingdom. Implications are drawn for language policies in developing countries.

Rosamaria Durand and Suzanne Deehy discuss the benefits and limitations of donated book programs in Chapter 9. They also outline procedures for ensuring that the strengths of the suppliers and the needs of the potential recipients are matched. They conclude that the goal of donated book programs should be to help countries develop local publishing efforts.

In the final chapter, Rebecca Knuth, Barbara Perry, and Brigitte Duces review the history of library support for literacy development. They outline the advantages and disadvantages of various delivery systems, including mobile libraries, rotating collections, village reading corners, and school libraries. The authors also describe the role of libraries in literacy programs in Tanzania, Thailand, Jamaica, Malaysia, and Nigeria.

Promoting Reading in Developing Countries should provide valuable information for governments of developing countries, government officials in education, teacher trainers in developing countries, reading professors, and publishers in developed and developing countries. The insights provided by the contributors to this volume, and the important recommendations they propose for the future, should add much to the discussion on how to make reading material more accessible and how to increase literacy levels—a necessary precondition for raising the quality of life in developing countries throughout the world.

1 | Reading in Developing Countries: Problems and Issues

Vincent Greaney

CLOSE TO 1 BILLION people in the world cannot read. The vast majority of these live in developing nations. Without the ability to read they are denied access to important information about health, social, cultural, and political issues as well as sources of pleasure and enrichment. Without a sizable literate population it is difficult for nations to develop the human resources necessary to create viable economies, essential services, and civil societies.

Crash adult literacy programs in developing countries have met with varying degrees of success and failure. Long-term political commitment, adequate resources, competent instructors and instruction, and postliteracy materials to achieve success in increasing literacy (Cairns, 1994; Wagner, 1991). Similarly at the primary school level, "quick fixes" or innovative pedagogic approaches alone are unlikely to be successful in increasing students' reading ability. The problem of illiteracy in developing countries is multifaceted and encompasses economic, educational, and cultural dimensions.

In this chapter I will focus on the principal reasons many young people in developing countries have not learned to read. These include inadequate health provisions, adverse home circumstances, and gender inequities. Particular attention is focused on the school, the traditional source for learning to read and write. I also will discuss problems associated with the provision of textbooks and sup-

5

plementary reading material. The chapter concludes with several recommendations for improving literacy rates in developing countries.

Data on Illiteracy

Each year the United Nations Educational, Scientific and Cultural Organization (UNESCO), which has been described as "the world's
premier source of international education statistics" (Puryear, 1995,
p. 81), publishes data on the extent of worldwide illiteracy. Data for
these reports are provided by national governments. However, the
quality of statistical data in education for countries that are not members of the Organization for Economic Cooperation and Development
(OECD) is poor. In many cases this is due to scarcity of financial resources, lack of a trained workforce, or bureaucratic incompetence. In
some countries civil and political strife makes the collection of data
impossible. The problem of reaching valid conclusions about the state
of international illiteracy is confounded by countries' using different
approaches to measure literacy, including individual self-assessment,
number of years of school completed, or the completion of a certain
stage of school. For example, Bangladesh has used three different definitions of literacy in recent decades (Greaney, Khandker, & Alam, in
preparation). Other problems relate to the use of different age ranges
to describe adults and to the exclusion of some minorities (Greaney,
1993b). Bearing these caveats in mind, let us turn our attention to the
available data on illiteracy.

Total Number of Illiterates

UNESCO data (Table 1) show that the total number of illiterates
aged 15 years and older in the world increased from 890.1 million in
1970 to 949.5 million in 1985. A marginal reduction (to 948.1 million)
in the total number of illiterates was recorded in 1990. A further decline is expected by the year 2000, at which stage it is predicted there
will be 935.4 million illiterates in the world.

Between 1970 and 1990 the population of the world increased by
approximately 55%. Considering this fact, when the numbers for illiteracy in each region are expressed as a percentage of that region's
population (as shown in the right hand columns in Table 1, and in

Table 1   Global Illiteracy for Adults Aged 15 Years and Older

	Adult Illiterates (in millions)				Illiteracy Rates (%)			
	1970	1985	1990	2000	1970	1985	1990	2000
Developing Countries (including)								
Sub-Saharan Africa	115.0	133.9	138.8	146.8	77.4	59.2	52.7	40.3
Arab States	49.7	58.6	61.1	65.5	73.5	54.5	48.7	38.0
Latin America/ Caribbean	43.0	44.6	43.9	41.7	26.2	17.7	15.3	11.5
East Asia	324.1	295.3	278.8	236.5	46.8	28.5	23.8	17.2
South Asia	302.3	374.8	398.1	437.1	68.7	57.8	53.9	45.9
Developed Countries	47.8	42.3	31.5	15.7	6.2	4.6	3.3	1.5
World Total	890.1	949.5	948.1	935.4	38.5	29.4	26.5	21.8

Note: Some countries are classified both as Sub-Saharan Africa and Arab States. Further, although some countries are not included in the subregions shown, statistics for those countries are incorporated in the world total.

From *Compendium of Statistics on Illiteracy*, by the United Nations Educational, Scientific and Cultural Organization, 1990, Paris: Author. Copyright 1990 by UNESCO. Adapted by permission.

Figure 1), a much more encouraging picture emerges. From 1970 to 2000 the total percentage of illiterates in the world is expected to decrease from 39% to 22%.

Regional Variation

The overwhelming majority of illiterates are found in three regions: South Asia, East Asia, and Sub-Saharan Africa. Four adjoining Asian countries account for close to two-thirds of the total illiterates in the world over age 15: India (29.7%), China (25.8%), Pakistan (4.4 %), and Bangladesh (4.2%). At the national level, the illiteracy rate in 1990 was highest for Burkina Faso (82%), Sierra Leone (79%), Benin (77%), Guinea-Bissau (76%), Nepal (74%), Sudan (73%), and the Gambia (73%).

Figure 1   Global Illiteracy for Adults Aged 15 Years and Older

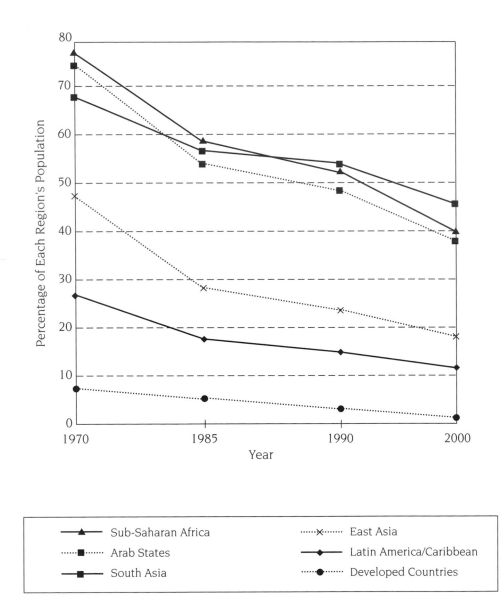

From *Compendium of Statistics on Illiteracy*, by the United Nations Educational, Scientific and Cultural Organization, 1990, Paris: Author. Copyright 1990 by UNESCO. Adapted by permission.

Age Variation

In all regions illiteracy rates in 1990 were highest for those aged 44 years and older (see Table 2). In both Sub-Saharan Africa and South Asia the illiteracy rate for those in the 15 to 19 age group was approximately half that of the 44+ age group. The most striking difference occurred in East Asia, where the rate of illiteracy among the 15 to 19 age group was less than one-eighth of that for the 44+ group, a reflection of the success of efforts to provide education in the region.

Gender Variation

National-level aggregate statistics mask large differences between the numbers of males and females who can read. The worldwide illiteracy rate is estimated at 19.4% for males and 33.6% for females; in developing countries the rate is at 25.1% and 45%, respectively. However, this level is much higher—40.9% for males and 67.8% for females—in South Asia alone. In all regions except Latin America and the Caribbean the illiteracy rate for females is over 50% greater than that for males (see Figure 2). The following countries had female illiteracy rates in excess of 80% in 1990: Afghanistan, Benin, Burkina Faso, Chad, Gambia, Guinea, Nepal, Niger, Sierra Leone, Somalia, and Sudan. In the two most populous countries, China and India, 50% of adult females are illiterate. The pattern of a higher illiteracy rate for females persists in other low-income countries as well as in middle- and even high-income countries.

Table 2 Illiteracy Rates in Developing Countries by Region and Age Group (%), 1990

Age Group	Sub-Saharan Africa	Arab States	Latin America/ Caribbean	East Asia	South Asia
15–19	35.9	27.7	6.2	6.3	37.7
20–24	40.3	32.9	7.6	8.5	42.3
25–44	55.5	48.5	12.7	16.8	53.1
44+	82.0	76.3	27.5	51.8	71.1

From *Compendium of Statistics on Illiteracy*, by the United Nations Educational, Scientific and Cultural Organization, 1990, Paris: Author. Copyright 1990 by UNESCO. Adapted by permission.

Figure 2   Illiteracy Rates in Developing Countries by Gender
             and Region

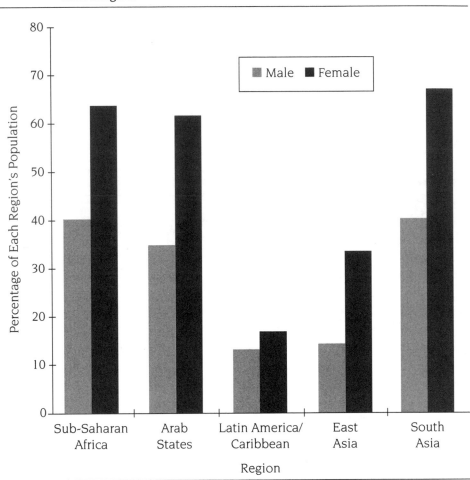

From *Compendium of Statistics on Illiteracy*, by the United Nations Educational, Scientific and Cultural
Organization, 1990, Paris: Author. Copyright 1990 by UNESCO. Adapted by permission.

Reasons for Illiteracy

Inadequate Health Provisions

Health, education, and literacy are closely interrelated. To become literate a person must survive the critical early years and be
healthy enough to benefit from formal and informal opportunities to

learn. However, mere survival is a problem in many developing countries. Presently 1 billion people, including more than 10% of the rural population in the Congo, Swaziland, and Paraguay, do not have access to clean water. A total of 1.7 billion poor people live without adequate sanitation; the diseases stemming from these conditions kill 2 to 3 million children annually (World Bank, 1993). In 1991 OECD countries reported infant mortality rates of 7 per 1,000 live births (World Bank, 1995e). The comparable figures for both China and India were 60, and for the other low-income countries 91 (down from 96 and 136, respectively, in 1970). In Mozambique, Sierra Leone, Malawi, and Mali, infant mortality rates exceeded 140 per 1,000 births in 1991. In 1990, 12.4 million children under age 5 died in the developing world. Had these countries experienced the same mortality rate as the developed world the number would have been 1.1 million (World Bank, 1993). The relation between health and literacy is underlined in the findings of a 100-country study that showed that a substantial increase in adult literacy rates would lead to a sharp increase in life expectancy and a pronounced reduction in infant mortality (Preston, 1985).

In impoverished countries, the capacity of children to learn is reduced by hunger, chronic malnutrition, micronutrient deficiencies, parasitic infections, and vision and hearing impairments (Levinger, 1994; Pollitt, 1990; World Bank, 1993). As many as 1 million children go blind each year from nutritional deficiency. Inadequately fed children also have poor attention spans and little energy for learning to read and write. Most recent data (World Bank, 1995d) indicate a very high incidence of malnutrition for children under age 5 for Bangladesh (68%) and India (63%), a key factor in accounting for the low literacy levels in these two countries. Currently around 184 million children of preschool age suffer from growth faltering due to a combination of factors such as insufficient diets and infectious diseases (World Bank, 1995b). In Thailand a 10% fall below the average height for age in the population corresponds to a 14% drop in grade attainment. Children with poor nutrition are also much less likely to enroll in school; a Nepalese study reported that the probability of a child's attending school was only 5% when he or she was 10% below the normal height for age for healthy children, compared with 27% for those at the norm (World Bank, 1993).

In recent decades the developing world has made substantial gains in health provision (World Bank, 1993). Over the past 40 years life expectancy has improved more than during the entire previous span of human history. In 1950 life expectancy in developing countries was 40 years. By 1990 it increased by more than 50% to 63 years. Many parts of the world, however, have not benefited from the overall general improvement in the quality of health provision. The lowest life expectancy rates (less than 50 years) have been recorded for Angola, Burkina Faso, Burundi, Central African Republic, Chad, Guinea, Mali, Mauritania, Mozambique, Niger, Rwanda, Senegal, Sierra Leone, Tanzania, and Uganda.

Basic education seems to lead to healthier families and enables parents to become better educators of their children, but the mechanism through which education and literacy work to improve health is unclear. For instance, it is not known to what extent health benefits arise directly from what is heard or seen at school or, subsequently, as a result of learning to read. Schooling seems important, in part, because it facilitates access to specific information about health benefits and risks (World Bank, 1993). People with more schooling better understand the consequences of not seeking care and are more articulate in their interactions with health-care providers. People who have learned to read can comprehend health-related information from newspapers, brochures, posters, books, and magazines. They also can decipher printed labels on agricultural products, including fertilizers and insecticides, and instructions on medicinal products. Reading printed instructions for using pharmaceutical products and agricultural chemicals was found to be one of the most common uses of school-acquired literacy and numeracy in a study carried out in several districts in Kenya (Eisemon, 1988). In addition, education can help counteract the influence of superstition. The people in India's rural villages who regard smallpox as a visitation of the Mother Goddess devote more time to worship and the performance of religious rites and rituals than to medical care of the patient (Mathur, 1993).

Female literacy is particularly relevant to health provision. First, in many countries, community health-care volunteers are an integral part of the primary health system. However, finding women to serve as volunteers has become a problem because literacy is often a prerequisite to service (Smith, 1994). Second, numerous studies confirm that mother's schooling has significantly greater effect on a child's health than does father's schooling. Surveys in 25 developing countries show that, all else being equal, one to three years of maternal schooling was associated with a 15% reduction in child mortality; a similar level of paternal schooling was associated with a 6% reduction (World Bank, 1993). In Peru, seven years of maternal schooling was associated with a nearly 75% reduction in mortality rate, about 28% more than the reduction for a similar level of paternal schooling (Hobcraft, 1993).

Adverse Home Circumstances

Research in developed countries (Adams, 1990; Guthrie & Siefert, 1984; Hess & Holloway, 1984; Ingham, 1982) has highlighted the contribution of the home to the development of prereading, vocabulary, and comprehension skills as well as to the development of positive reading habits and attitudes. Once the ability to read fluently has been mastered, whether a young person develops the reading habit depends to a great extent on home attitudes and circumstances (Gopinathan, 1978; Guthrie & Greaney, 1991; Southgate, Arnold, & Johnson, 1981; Spiegel, 1981). The 32-school system 1992 International Association for the Evaluation of Educational Achievement (IEA) Study of Reading Literacy, which included some developing countries, investigated the relation between reading achievement and a range of variables including school and teacher factors (see also Elley's Chapter 2 in this volume). The study identified home environment as "the single most critical factor in the development of literacy" (Lundberg & Linnakyla, 1993, p. 93). The study also showed that amount of voluntary reading and number of reading materials in the home were positively correlated with reading achievement (Elley, 1994). In a separate analysis of the Indonesian data from the IEA study, characteristics of students' homes proved to be important predictors of reading behavior and achievement at both the primary and secondary levels (Greaney, 1993a).

Home factors that militate against the development of literacy in developing countries include illiterate parents and elders in the home, reticence about encouraging reading in the home, lack of appropriate reading material, inability of parents to purchase any form of reading material, lack of space and light, number of household chores, child labor practices, and in some instances, communal lifestyles which frown on solitary activities such as reading (Greaney, 1986). Unlike their counterparts in more affluent countries, children in developing countries are unlikely to be confronted regularly with printed matter in the home in newspapers and magazines, on covers of boxes and wrappings, on television screens, and outside in the forms of billboards and public signs; these latter "exposure-to-print" factors have been identified as important independent contributors to the development of reading skills (Cunningham & Stanovich, 1991).

Gender Inequities

A major reason for illiteracy among females in developing countries is that school participation rates for females are almost always lower than those for males (UNESCO, 1994). In 1992, for every 100 boys at each level, there were 80 primary school girls and 67 secondary school girls in low-income countries (World Bank, 1995e). The proportion of girls in primary schools has been increasing gradually in recent decades. In 1990, the average 6-year-old girl in low- and middle-income countries could expect to attend school for 7.7 years; a similar aged boy could expect to attend for 9.3 years (World Bank, 1995c). This differential in expected attendance is greatest (2.9 years) in South Asia (the only region where it is not decreasing) and in the Middle East (2.1 years). Among adults the differential between males and females in the amount of schooling received is more pronounced. Extremely high numbers of females—up to 90% of females over age 25 in some instances (UNESCO, 1994)—have not received schooling in many developing countries.

Reasons for the lower school participation rate of girls in developing areas vary from country to country and can be attributed to a combination of cultural and economic circumstances. In some countries deep-rooted attitudes operate against girls almost from the moment of birth (Ramadas, 1994). Many parents simply do not appreciate the value of educating their daughters; others are concerned with the safety of their girls en route to school and while at school. In Pakistan's largest province, Baluchistan, boys have enrolled in schools in greater numbers because 90% of the schools are designated for boys (World Bank, 1995a). The direct and indirect costs of educating daughters are also a concern for parents. For example, school fees may be too ex-

To improve literacy rates among females in developing countries, governments and nongovernmental organizations should develop specific programs to ensure that more girls enroll and persist in primary school and that more female teachers are trained. © Paud Murphy. Used by permission.

pensive for low-income parents. School attire frequently costs more for girls than for boys (Chowdhury, 1993). Further, the opportunity costs (the costs incurred by a family due to loss of the child's help in the home or on the farm and, in some instances, loss of income from the child working outside the home) of educating girls tend to be higher than for boys. Girls (especially the eldest girl) help supervise younger siblings and do chores such as farming, fetching firewood and water, and cooking. In some instances truancy from school can be attributed to the neglect of girls' health and nutritional needs (King & Hill, 1993). Also, literature, folklore, and religious texts in many cultures abound with observations of the inferiority of women.

Girls in developing countries tend to marry young, frequently in their early teens. Both in developed and developing countries, teenage marriage is associated with early withdrawal from school (Alan Guttmacher Institute, 1995). Another reason for the lower school par-

ticipation rate of girls in some countries is that a girl is not considered as good an educational investment as a boy because she becomes part of her husband's family. Parents assume they can depend
on their son to support them in their old age. Many parents also consider that delaying marriage because of schooling will delay receipt of
the bride's wealth and may even reduce its amount if greater value is
placed on younger rather than better educated brides (King & Hill,
1993). In addition, cultural norms in some countries dictate that
women will not fit into traditional roles if they become educated
(Bequele & Boyden, 1988).

The arguments in favor of educating girls are strong. A review of
evidence led Summers (1994) to conclude that enrolling girls in
school was probably the single most effective antipoverty policy in
the developing world today. Raising the level of women's education
is related to later age of marriage; later start of family; lower risks to
the child's and mother's health; improved hygiene, nutrition, and im-
munization practices; increased knowledge about health; higher productivity (Herz et al., 1991; Wolfensohn, 1995; World Bank, 1993);
higher educational attainment of both sons and daughters; improved
environment (Sandstrom, 1995); and smaller family size (Cochrane,
O'Hara, & Leslie, 1980). Additional schooling for females is associated with reduction in fertility and infant mortality, as mentioned earlier (World Bank, 1993). In Sub-Saharan Africa, secondary schooling is
universally associated with lower fertility, and the effect increases
with additional years of schooling (Ainsworth, Beegle, & Nyamete,
1995). Educating girls also increases the potential for females to acquire positions of influence at local, regional, and national levels,
which eventually can lead to initiatives, programs, and policies designed to improve the provision and quality of education for girls
(Wolfensohn, 1995).

Adverse School Factors

It is difficult to learn to read without attending formal school.
The completion of four grades of primary education is considered a
prerequisite for children to become literate (UNESCO, 1990a). Evidence from Bangladesh indicates that the completion of grade four
marked the point at which the majority was able to attain low-level

competency in reading (Greaney, Khandker, & Alam, in preparation). A Brazilian study established that the average person must attend school for three to four years before formal education has an impact on national economic growth (Lau et al., 1993). Until recent years, the challenge for developing countries has been to build schools and ensure that children attend. Despite severe economic hardships, developing countries have greatly improved the provision of basic primary education. Between 1965 and 1989, primary school enrollment rates increased by more than 40% in the two largest low-income countries, China and India, and by more than 50% in other low-income countries. Between 1970 and 1990, impressive improvements in global gross enrollment rates for primary school (GERP) have been recorded (see Figure 3). (Gross enrollment is the ratio of children of all ages en-

Figure 3   Percentage of Primary-Age Group Enrolled in Education Based on Gross Enrollment Ratios

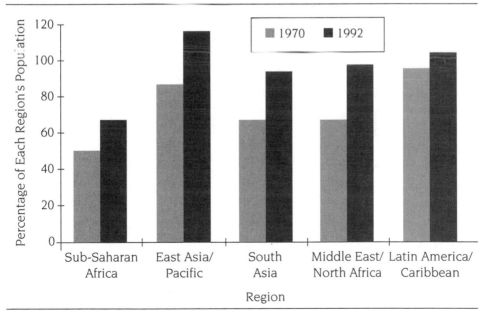

Note: The gross enrollment ratio is the total number of students in primary school divided by the population of the primary school age group. It can include students who are younger or older than the country's standard primary school age.

Adapted from *World Development Report*, by the World Bank, 1995, Washington, DC: Author.

rolled in primary school to the country's population of school-age children. The ratio takes into account students who are older or younger than the country's standard primary school age). However, Sub-Saharan Africa and to a lesser extent South Asia are still far from attaining universal primary education.

Nonattendance. The number of school-age children in developing countries who never enrolled or who enrolled and subsequently withdrew from school amounted to 129 million in 1990 and is estimated to be 162 million by 2015 (UNESCO, 1993). In Africa, where the problem is most severe and getting worse, 50% of all primary school-age children are out of school (World Bank, 1995c). Although the total number of students increased by over one-third, the percentage of 6- to 11-year-olds in school dropped by close to 4% between 1980 and 1992 (UNESCO, 1994). The out-of-school percentage for Africa is almost twice the rate for South Asia (27%) and for the Middle East (24%). At the moment, 12 countries in Africa and South Asia (including Pakistan and Ethiopia) have GERPs of less than 50% (World Bank, 1995c). In sharp contrast, only two Latin American and Caribbean countries, Guatemala (79%) and Bolivia (81%), recorded a GERP of less than 95%.

Poor attendance. Even if a child is enrolled in school, without regular attendance it is almost impossible for him or her to acquire mastery of basic literacy skills. Factors that have contributed to low attendance rates or early withdrawal from school in some countries include a shortage of accessible schools and lack of parent interest in education. Poor school attendance is associated with children with special needs; rural, linguistic, or ethnic minorities; refugees; and street children. Parents' having to pay fees or supplemental charges for primary schools has been a disincentive for educating children in some countries (World Bank, 1995c) as have the high opportunity costs of sending children to school, especially at the senior primary levels. As mentioned earlier, many parents require their children to work from an early age to supplement the family income. For instance, India has an estimated 44 million child laborers. In Pakistan children between ages 10 and 14 account for 10% of the entire workforce (Weiner, 1991). To cite another example, Nigeria has 12 million child workers and Brazil 7 million (International Labor Office, 1992). If children work outside the home instead of attend school, they contribute more than they consume, unlike the situation in developed countries (Siddiqi & Patrinos, 1995). Parents must become convinced that attendance at school is of sufficient value to compensate for lost earnings.

Noncompletion. In South Asia and Latin America and the Caribbean, approximately 30% of children do not complete second grade. The limited available evidence (UNESCO, 1990a) suggests that fewer than 80% in East Asia complete fourth grade. The situation is much worse in the remaining regions: in 1986 between 55% and 66% completed fourth grade. In Brazil, out of 1,000 children entering school, only 330 reach the end of basic schooling (eighth grade) and take an average of 12 years to do so (Torres, 1994). In all developing countries about 30% who enroll in primary school do not complete the final grade (World Bank, 1995c).

Repetition. Unless a student learns more by repeating a grade, repetition tends to be an expensive exercise. High levels of grade repetition are features of some school systems. In Latin America, 50% of students repeat first grade (Torres, 1994). Although some repetition is to be expected for reasons such as illness or low achievement, the relatively high levels reported for some countries are a cause for concern. In a 14-country African study, repeaters as a percentage of the total primary school enrollment ranged from 2% for Zambia to as high as 29% for Madagascar and 35% for Togo. Also, the rate of repetition for Francophone countries studied was approximately four times that for Anglophone countries (Kellaghan & Greaney, 1992). Repetition is often a precursor to dropping out of school early.

Inadequate School Instruction

Many children in developed countries acquire essential prereading skills (partly through being read to) and in some instances reading skills (such as letter- and word-identification skills) through interactions in the home prior to attending school, as mentioned earlier. Because this level of home support is not as likely to occur in many developing countries, children have to depend on teachers for basic instruction to a greater extent than do their counterparts in developed countries. However, by the standards of industrialized countries, teachers in developing countries tend to be poorly qualified (Lockheed et al., 1991).

Teacher training. In developing countries entry requirements for teacher training programs, and as a result subject-level knowledge, tend to be low. In Madagascar as little as five years of formal schooling was the highest entry requirement for admission into teacher training (Zymelman & De Stefano, 1989). Students in many developing countries may opt for teacher training after completing no more than the junior cycle, which is usually three years, of secondary school. Among low-income countries in Asia, students can commence teacher-training programs as young as 15 (in Pakistan and China) and 16 (in Bangladesh and India). Perhaps as a result of low entry requirements, in 1993 it was estimated that at least 700,000 primary school teachers in China were unqualified (Sun & Deng, 1995).

In addition, teacher training tends to be inadequate. In Somalia, Thailand, Northern Yemen, and the Philippines, less than 15% of the curriculum is devoted to developing pedagogical skills such as methods of teaching reading. In some countries the low level of student achievement in primary and secondary school means that the first two years of teacher training is spent on secondary school skills instruction. For instance, in Zimbabwe, despite some impressive improvements in teacher training provision, in 1983 about 10% of trained primary school teachers had no secondary school education (Kelly, 1991). Training in Zimbabwe also has been criticized for "its unimaginative teaching style that emphasizes factual knowledge, memorization, and convergent thinking" (Kelly, 1991, p. 133).

Subject-level mastery. In developing countries the dedication and professionalism of many teachers enables them to overcome their adverse teaching situations. Many others, however, often lack the intellectual skills to function effectively in the classroom. Teachers' knowledge of subject matter, an established predictor of student achievement (World Bank, 1995c), is frequently lacking. In the Philippines teachers have been found to perform no better than their students on external achievement tests (Philippines, The Congressional Commission on Education, 1993). Teacher trainees in Pakistan correctly answered about half of questions based on the content of the fifth-grade primary school curriculum in mathematics and science (Robinson, 1995). National and local politicians, prompted by the prospect of personal or political gain, occassionally have disregarded official procedures and appointed unqualified teachers, including illiterate teachers, thereby contributing to the low level of subject mastery in many instances.

Morale. Teacher morale in developing countries tends to be low, which generally can be attributable to salaries that are often below the poverty line. One report described African primary teachers as "often a beleaguered and dispirited force, their status much eroded and their working conditions poor" (World Bank, 1988, p. 41). Absence of teachers, frequently dictated by the need to supplement meager incomes by taking additional teaching positions, is commonplace (Lockheed et al., 1991). These teacher absences, combined with disruptions and unscheduled closings, reduce the amount of time available for students to develop and practice reading and writing skills.

Class size. Although the research literature in general does not indicate that large classes contribute to lower reading achievement scores (Harbison & Hanushek, 1992; Lundberg & Linnakyla, 1992), classes in some developing countries are too large to incorporate small-group or individualized instruction or to share limited resources such as supplementary readers. The average class size for low-income countries has been estimated at 39 students. In South Asia it is as high as 61 (World Bank, 1995d). Primary school student-teacher ratios in excess of 60 have been recorded for Bangladesh, Burundi, Central African Republic, Chad, Congo, India, and Malawi, whereas the student-teacher ratios for some developed countries are much lower: Sweden (10), Austria and Denmark (11), France (12), Germany and Norway (16), Canada (17), and the United States and Japan (20) (World Bank, 1995d).

Teaching methods. Teaching in many impoverished countries tends to be of the "chalk-and-talk" variety with a high priority being placed on the acquisition of basic skills. Much use is made of the chalkboard (Lockheed et al., 1991). Discussions with the teacher or among small groups of students, encouragement of risk taking, and questioning of the material being presented—important factors in the development of language and reading skills—tend not to be encouraged (Pfau, 1980). In the IEA Study of Reading Literacy, there was a tendency for teachers from developing countries to emphasize reading skills, whereas the development of positive reading habits and attitudes was given higher priority by teachers from the higher scoring developed countries (Lundberg & Linnakyla, 1992).

Functions of reading. Perhaps because of teachers' emphasis on skills as opposed to reading for pleasure, children in a number of developing countries tend to view reading in terms of functional or utilitarian purposes, such as helping to pass examinations (Greaney & Neuman, 1990). Relatively little emphasis is placed on reading for pleasure, a consistent positive predictor of reading achievement in both developed and developing countries (Anderson, Wilson, & Fielding, 1988; Elley, 1992, 1994; Greaney, 1980). This also may be attributed to the inaccessibility of interesting supplementary reading material; in the IEA Study of Reading Literacy, students in developing countries were much less likely to have access to bookstores or to have a supply of books in their homes than their counterparts from more affluent countries (Elley, 1992). (See also the section "Lack of Reading Materials" in this chapter.)

Achievement standards. Valid comparative student reading achievement data are rare, although the limited available evidence suggests that reading achievement levels of students in developing countries are below those of students in OECD countries (Lockheed et al., 1991). Only two developing countries participated in an early IEA literature education study (Purves, 1973) and three in an IEA reading comprehension study (Thorndike, 1973). Test performances of those in developing countries who participated in the 1992 IEA Reading Literacy Study (Elley, 1994) tended to be poor by the standards of OECD countries and, in most instances, were below the expected performance levels after allowance had been made for the country's state of development. Two Brazilian studies found that students' performance levels were considerably lower than those set by local experienced educators (Harbison & Hanushek, 1992; Torres, 1994).

Lack of Reading Materials

Books are essential, especially where teacher mastery of subject matter is weak and students do not have access to modern technologies. Teachers seldom have access to national curriculum guidelines and have to depend on the textbook in determining what specific content areas should be covered. Although the research on school effectiveness in developing countries is far from clear (Hanushek, 1995), access to textbooks has been identified as one of the most effective means of raising school achievement (Hanushek, 1995; Heyneman & Loxley, 1983; Kremer, 1995; Lundberg & Linnakyla, 1992). The importance of textbook availability in the 1992 IEA study was underscored by the significant positive correlation recorded between number of textbooks per student and reading achievement in Hungary, Indonesia, Trinidad and Tobago, and Zimbabwe (Lundberg & Linnakyla, 1992).

Textbook shortage. Data on number of textbooks per student are rare, but available evidence suggests that there is a textbook shortage in developing countries. Terms such as "textbook famine" have been used to describe the lack of textbooks in Africa. In Uganda, in 1970, there was an average of one book for every three primary school students; by 1980 it had slipped to one per twelve students (Farrell & Heyneman, 1989). In the IEA Reading Literacy Study, students from developing countries, with the notable exceptions of Botswana and Hungary, tended to have fewer than one textbook each, far fewer than their counterparts from developed countries (Lundberg & Linnakyla, 1992).

The shortage of textbooks can be attributed to a number of factors (Altbach, 1992; de Guzman, 1989; Farrell & Heyneman, 1989; Greaney 1993b; Kats & Pacheo, 1992; "Problems," 1994). Due to poor economic growth there is a very low consumer demand for books. Parents simply cannot afford to buy them; in China, for example, the high cost of textbooks probably has contributed to the inability of some parents to send their children to school (Beemer, 1996). Textbook production in developing countries involves many problems unlikely to be encountered in the developed world. For example, textbook publishing and production tend to be handled by the state. Like many nationalized efforts in developing countries, government departments charged with book production are frequently bureaucratic and inefficient. Centralized efforts to publish textbooks also have had serious negative consequences for local publishers. Denied access to the more lucrative textbook market, these publishers are not in a position to produce interesting fiction and nonfiction material for young readers. Nongovernment publishers also struggle to gain access to capital. A lack of foreign exchange makes the purchase of printing machinery and paper difficult. Paper, which tends to be supplied by a relatively small number of countries, is expensive and its supply uncertain. In many smaller countries, book print runs tend to be small; thus publishers are unable to benefit from the economies of scale experienced by those who cater to the major language groups in larger countries. Another concern is that writing and editorial skills are in short supply. Overall textbook quality in terms of both content and production remains low. Other problems related to textbook publishing in developing countries include poor management, unfavorable climatic conditions, and book distribution difficulties due to inadequate storage facilities, poor transportation and communication systems, and high costs in remote areas. In addition, booksellers find it difficult to establish credit with publishers and suppliers and thus tend to limit their stocks. (The difficulties of textbook publishing and production are discussed in detail in Chapters 4 and 5.)

Language factors. Research findings suggest that initial instruction should be offered in a child's first language. After two to three years of instruction in this language a child can learn a second language fairly effectively provided he or she is given many opportunities in the classroom to speak the language and the teacher speaks the second language well (Clay, 1993). However, the complexity of the language policies and practices in developing countries makes following these instructional guidelines difficult. Consider the following example. In the Northwest Frontier Province in Pakistan, a child may speak one of a variety of local languages at home. Because of political pressure from certain groups the language of instruction in about half the districts is Pushto, while the others learn in the official national language, Urdu. Instruction in the higher grades and major examinations are given in Urdu. Students who undertake their early instruction in Pushto are at a decided disadvantage in these examinations. If given the opportunity, parents would prefer their children have instruction in English because they believe that it will lead to greater employment opportunities and benefits.

The IEA Reading Literacy Study found that students whose home language differed from the school language performed less well on the reading tests than those who were tested in their home language (Elley, 1994). In many developing countries, however, it is simply economically impossible to publish materials in the students' home language. Zambia, with a population of less than 9 million, has seven principal languages (each spoken by at least 10% of the country's population) and five official languages (World Bank, 1988). India has 1,652 mother tongues and "between 200 and 700 languages belonging to four language families, (and) ten major writing systems..." (Pattanyak, 1993, pp. 50–51). China has seven basic language groups; Hann Chinese, usually called Chinese, has upwards of 1,000 dialects. A number of languages do not have alphabets. Because of these differences the language of instruction is usually a highly emotive political issue. Changes in government can lead to shifts in language policy. Publishing textbooks for each of the major linguistic groups adds considerably to national textbook production costs and may have major budgetary implications for educational administrators.

Newspapers. Besides providing the major source of news information, newspapers allow people to exercise their literacy skills. Newspaper circulation figures (per 1,000 population), which are estimated at 320 and 125 for high- and middle-income countries respectively, are much lower in developing countries, where the figures range from 85 for Latin American and Caribbean countries, to 33 for the Middle East and North Africa, to 26 for South Asia, and to 12 for Sub-Saharan Africa. Countries with circulation figures of one or less per 1,000 include Burkina Faso, Central African Republic, Chad, Mauritania, Niger, Rwanda, and Swaziland (World Bank, 1995d).

Supplementary reading material. Broad reading of self-selected material is associated with acquisition of vocabulary and comprehension skills and the development of the reading habit (Guthrie & Greaney, 1991; Lundberg & Linnakyla, 1992; Postlethwaite & Ross, 1992). In developing countries, the general dearth of reading material is most pronounced in the area of books other than textbooks. As mentioned, students are less likely to have access to public libraries and bookstores than their counterparts in developed countries (Ross & Postlethwaite, 1994). Supplementary reading materials that meet students' interests are rarely found in classrooms in developing countries. Apart from the general unavailability of funds and the high unit costs of books, other factors that contribute to the shortage of materials are lack of local booksellers, publishers, and writers of children's literature, and teacher discomfort with students' reading material that is not on an examination or in the curriculum.

Increasing efforts are being made to introduce students in developing countries to material other than textbooks. Many countries have introduced innovative programs to promote a love for reading and the reading habit. In Indonesia, to cite one example, a large range of titles have been funded, produced, and distributed by the government. The contents of some of the books, however, have been criticized for their failure to reflect children's interests (Bunanta, 1993). In many developing countries it may not be possible to obtain interesting reading material in the first language, either locally produced or in the form of imports. Also, the subject matter and illustrations in many imported books are often unfamiliar to the cultural backgrounds of young readers (Alemna, 1982; Osa, 1986). International donors also support supplementary reading projects usually as part of larger projects in a range of countries, including Malaysia, Brazil, Tanzania, Nigeria, Ethiopia, and Eritrea (Buchan, 1995). Unfortunately, innovations of this type tend to falter in times of financial constraint.

Book donation schemes. In the absence of locally produced supplementary material for children and adults, schools and governments have on occasion used international book donation schemes (see Chapter 9). Donated material can serve the needs of certain audiences, especially advanced students in technical and language subject areas. However, the language and frequently the content of donated materials may render them unsuitable for most young readers and nonspecialist readers. For example, in visits to primary school libraries in disadvantaged areas of the Philippines, I have seen English books by John Ruskin and Thomas Carlyle and one in French by Gustave Flaubert, whereas in village libraries in Indonesia I have seen manuals for an American car, one for servicing an airplane, and another for completing a United States income tax form.

Literacy and Human Development

As mentioned, economically developed countries scored much higher on three separate reading tests than the small number of developing countries that participated in the IEA Reading Literacy Study. For example, Finnish 14-year-old students answered correctly almost three times as many items as their counter parts in Botswana (see Elley, Chapter 2). The reading score difference between the developed and the developing countries is not surprising considering the literacy-related advantages of the wealthier countries such as more schools, textbooks, and libraries; healthier children; and interested parents.

Using the World Bank's *Social Indicators of Development* (1995d) database for each developing country for which data were available (64 out of a total of 78 countries; key data were not available for some countries including Cambodia, Cuba, Ethiopia, Malawi, Nicaragua, South Africa, and Vietnam), I investigated the relation between level of development and reading *within* developing countries. Some additional data were obtained from United Nations Development Program (1994), UNESCO (1990b, 1992), and World Bank (1993). The analyses was limited to countries with mean gross national products (GNP) per capita of US$3,830 or lower (the mean overall GNP per capita of these countries was US$1,050). The selected variables were GNP per capita; gross enrollment rate for primary school (GERP) (the percentage of all children enrolled in primary school expressed as a percentage of the population in the age range catered to by the primary school); gross enrollment rate for secondary school (GERS); life expectancy; low birth weight; and newspapers per 1,000 of the population (see Table 3). GNP provided an economic indicator of a country's wealth. It also provided a measure of a country's ability to pay for health and education services. Enrollment rates for schools provided an indication of school availability and the country's perception of the value of education. The two health indicators, life expectancy and birth weight, provided measures of the general level of national health. Number of newspapers per 1,000 suggested the value placed on literacy in the country. Because very few of the countries had participated in comparative reading literacy surveys, literacy rate was used as a proxy for reading achievement.

Four variables—gross enrollment for primary school, gross enrollment for secondary school, newspaper production, and life expectancy—correlate highly (over .6) with the reported literacy rate. Together the set of variables account for 81.5% of the variance in literacy. They present evidence of a strong association between the extent of human development (specifically economic, education, and health) within a developing country and reading achievement levels as represented by literacy rate. (Data for the six indicators were combined to create an index of human development. The lower ranking countries on this index were, in order, Niger, Bangladesh, Sierra Leone, Mali,

Table 3 Correlations Among Economic, School, Health, and Literacy Indicators in 64 Selected Underdeveloped Countries

	1.	2.	3.	4.	5.	6.	7.
1. GNP per capita (US$)	1.00						
2. Enrollment in primary school	0.50	1.00					
3. Enrollment in secondary school	0.59	0.72	1.00				
4. Life expectancy in years	0.59	0.68	0.68	1.00			
5. Birth weight	0.37	0.19	0.21	0.22	1.00		
6. Newspaper circulation per 1,000 population	0.70	0.34	0.54	0.46	0.29	1.00	
7. Literacy at age 15	0.63	0.74	0.71	0.76	0.40	0.57	1.00

Adapted from *Social Indicators of Development*, by the World Bank, 1995, Washington, DC: Author.

Burkina Faso, Pakistan, Guinea, Guinea-Bissau, and Rwanda. There was virtually no change in country rank order when illiteracy rate was included in the index).

Recommendations for Improving Literacy Rates

Much has been achieved in raising international reading literacy standards. In the last 20 years there has been a drop in the official illiteracy rate data in the 15- to 24-year age group, most likely due to a sharp increase in school enrollment figures in all parts of the world. Over the last 30 years progress in the area of health, through the provision of cleaner water, better nutrition, and improved health services, has been even more pronounced and has helped halve the proportion of children dying before age 5 (World Bank, 1993). However, as the world's population continues to increase, it is estimated that there will be at least 900 million illiterates by the year 2000, and the overwhelming majority of these will be in South Asia, Sub-Saharan Africa, and the Arab States (UNESCO, 1990b).

Development (in the form of economic, health, and education improvement) and literacy are highly correlated. Governments with little or no resources do not have the capacity to develop their educational and health sectors. As national economies develop, governments are better able to divert resources to health services, teacher salaries and training, schools and libraries, and textbooks and supplementary reading material, and to restrict child labor practices, all of which increase the likelihood that children will learn to read.

A young population who can read is a necessary condition for economic growth. In the past, economic development was dependent on the availability of physical resources such as land and mineral wealth. The modern world requires human resource development. Gary Becker (1995), Nobel-prize winner for economics in 1992, observed that the primary determinant of a country's standard of living is how well it succeeds in *developing* and *utilizing* the skills, knowledge, health, and habits of its population. The World Bank's heavy investment in education (currently about US$2 billion per annum) is based on the assumption that investment in people is vital if poverty is to be reduced and economic and human development to occur.

The following strategies are likely to lead to a substantial improvement in reading literacy rates.

Invest in Education

Raising educational standards requires additional government expenditure on education in general and on the primary school sector in particular. Unfortunately, the limited evidence suggests that between 1980 and 1990, per student expenditure fell in about half of the developing countries for which data were available (UNESCO, 1993). In many developing countries expenditure on defense accounts for only slightly less than the combined health and education budgets [for instance, Africa has 83 soldiers for every doctor; more affluent countries have 4 ("Peddling," 1994)]. For countries with low primary school enrollment, resources should be directed to the primary sector where the majority of students are found.

Improve Basic Education Provision

Primary school enrollment can be increased by constructing schools in areas where children do not have access to educational facilities, reducing the opportunity costs of schooling, providing textbooks and supplementary readers, introducing a more flexible school year to take into account the seasonal demands on child labor (in countries such as China and Colombia), introducing multiple shifts in schools by using the same school building to accommodate two to three different groups of students during the course of the day (in Philippines for example), and establishing daycare centers so that girls are not required to take care of their younger siblings (Chowdhury, 1995).

Improve Teacher Training and Teaching

The present general substandard level of teaching can be improved by attracting better students for teacher training, enhancing salaries, providing relevant preservice and inservice teacher training to meet the expressed needs of teachers, and regularly monitoring and evaluating teaching performance in classrooms. Politicians and administrators must desist from appointing people (frequently illiterates) to teaching posts when more qualified candidates are available.

Teachers should be introduced to sound pedagogical approaches for teaching reading through long- and short-term inservice programs, which can be provided through various means including distance education. In addition to letter- and word-identification skills, teaching of reading should emphasize the ability to read different forms of texts (including narrative prose such as fictional stories, expository prose designed to describe or explain something, and documents such as charts, labels, and forms) and the development of critical and analytical skills. Students should be given time to read in class to develop not only reading skills but also favorable reading habits and attitudes. Teachers must appreciate that learning is most likely to occur when the student is reading meaningful material for a purpose. Teachers should serve as reading role models by reading themselves and by sharing some of their reading experiences with their students. Reading instruction should also incorporate substantial amounts of student oral

The quality of teaching in developing countries can be improved by attracting better students for teacher training, enhancing salaries, providing better training, and regularly monitoring and evaluating teaching performance. © Skjold Photographs.

work and writing. Where possible, the visual dullness that is so much a feature of many classrooms in developing countries should be replaced by colorful inexpensive or gratis materials.

Create a Favorable Environment for Publishing

Governments must help create conditions that encourage the publication of textbooks and supplementary reading materials. With the exception of decisions about textbook content, much of the broad range of publishing activities including writing, printing, and distribution can be entrusted, or at least open to the private sector. Private and state publishers should be able to compete at the same level. In the interests of equity, state publishers should have the additional role of addressing the book needs of minority groups by publishing books for those studying minority subjects and distributing books to remote areas. Colombia's 1993 law ("New Book Law," 1995) provides a good example of positive governmental support for reading. Books were exempted from sales and value-added taxes, paper for book production from import taxes, and some authors from income taxes. Provision also was made to create and equip libraries.

Promote the Development of Independent Reading

Governments should support and encourage the provision of supplementary reading materials, which are essential for developing reading skills as well as positive reading habits and attitudes among young children. Support should be reflected in the content of pre- and inservice teacher-training courses, in the provision of interesting reading materials, and in the development of school and local libraries.

Promote the Education of Girls

Governments, nongovernmental organizations, and donor agencies should develop specific programs to ensure that more girls enroll and persist in primary school and that more female teachers are trained. Governments also can introduce more gender equity into public expenditure in education, which is lower for females in every region of the world. [The differential is most notable in the poorer regions; for example, the ratio of female to male expenditure is as low as .52 in

South and West Asia compared to .93 in developed countries (Schultz, 1993).] Some headway in this area has been made in recent years. A number of promising program initiatives supported by the World Bank and other donor agencies might be replicated. These include specific components to educate girls such as providing additional school places for girls (in Chad, Yemen, Pakistan, India, Senegal, and Bangladesh); building single-sex schools; establishing quota systems for girls (in Malawi and Tanzania); protecting girls' privacy and security by building toilets (Bangladesh) and school boundary walls (Pakistan); lowering direct costs by waiving or reducing fees for girls, offering scholarships for girls in rural areas (Bangladesh and Guatemala), and providing free textbooks, childcare centers, and flexible school hours (China, Colombia, Bangladesh, and India); lowering entry requirements for preservice teacher training (Pakistan); modifying home technology to reduce the burden on women in the home or the amount of time needed to collect wood (Nepal); sponsoring public relations campaigns in support of education (Pakistan, Morocco, and Papua New Guinea), and providing school feeding programs (Chowdhury, 1995; O'Grady, 1994; Sandstrom, 1995; World Bank, 1995a). Government attention can also be directed to removing gender bias in textbooks (King & Hill, 1993).

A Final Word

History offers good examples of why governments should be both patient and hopeful as they develop policies and programs to improve literacy rates. In one country as recently as 1900, life expectancy was 49 years, a figure that is substantially lower than the current average of 62 years for low-income countries worldwide. In this country parents kept large numbers of elementary school-age children at home because of their economic value. The average annual school attendance for 5- to 17-year-olds was 99 days. The country, the world's richest at that time, was the United States (Schultz, 1971). Even more pertinent in the present context has been the experience in Korea, a country devoid of natural resources and now one of Asia's most successful economies. In 1945 about 30% of children aged 6 to 11 were enrolled in school. The illiteracy rate in the 12+ population was 78%. Now after decades of intense investment and sound management of education, the enrollment rate for high school (ages 15 to 18) is well over 90%, and the adult illiteracy rate is less than 4% (Office for Standards in Education, 1994; Sorensen, 1994).

Persistent, focused, informed programs; courageous political leadership; good management of limited resources; and informed, enthusiastic teaching are required if we are to achieve the long-term goal of helping children in developing countries learn to read. When this goal is realized, these children will have access to new sources of knowledge, insights, and pleasure that can help illuminate and change the quality of their lives.

References

Adams, M.J. (1990). *Beginning to read: Thinking and learning about print.* Cambridge, MA: MIT Press.

Ainsworth, M., Beegle, K., & Nyamete, A. (1995). *The impact of female schooling on fertility and contraceptive use* (Living Standards Measurement Study, Working Paper No. 110). Washington, DC: World Bank.

Alan Guttmacher Institute. (1995). *Hopes and realities: Closing the gap between women's aspirations and their reproductive experiences.* New York: Author.

Alemna, A.A. (1982). Factors affecting the reading habits of African children. *School Librarian, 30,* 107–111.

Altbach, P.G. (Ed.). (1992). *Publishing and development in the third world.* London: Hans Zell.

Anderson, R.C., Wilson, P.T., & Fielding, L.G. (1988). Growth in reading and how children spend their time outside of school. *Reading Research Quarterly, 23,* 285–303.

Becker, G.S. (1995). *Human capital and poverty alleviation* (Human Resources Development and Operations Policy Working Paper No. 52). Washington, DC: World Bank.

Beemer, H. (1996, March). *Textbooks: Lessons from Asia: China.* Paper presented at World Bank Seminar, Washington, DC.

Bequele, A., & Boyden, J. (1988). Working children: Current trends and policy responses. *International Labor Review, 127,* 153–171.

Buchan, A. (1995). *Books and information for schools in the developing world.* Paper presented at the International Book Development/International Federation of Library Services Seminar, Harrogate, UK.

Bunanta, M. (1993, January 2). Inpres children's books: Should this be continued? *Kompas Daily,* 5.

Cairns, J.C. (1994). Lessons from past literacy campaigns: A critical assessment. In Z. Morsy (Ed.), *The challenge of illiteracy: From reflection to action* (pp. 105–114). New York: Garland.

Chowdhury, K.P. (1993). *Barriers and solutions to closing the gender gap* (Human Resources Development and Operations Policy Dissemination Notes No. 18). Washington, DC: World Bank.

Chowdhury, K.P. (1995). *Literacy and primary education* (Human Resources Development and Operations Policy Working Paper No. 50). Washington, DC: World Bank.

Clay, M. (1993). Language policy and literacy learning. In L. Limage (Ed.), *Language policy, literature, and culture* (pp. 31–40). Paris: United Nations Educational, Scientific and Cultural Organization.

Cochrane, S., O'Hara, D.J., & Leslie, J. (1980). *The effects of education on health* (World Bank Staff Working Paper No. 405). Washington, DC: World Bank.

Cunningham, A.E., & Stanovich, K.E. (1991). Tracking the unique effects of print exposure in children: Associations with vocabulary, general knowledge, and spelling. *Journal of Educational Psychology, 83,* 264–274.

de Guzman, A. (1989). The Philippines: A textbook case. In J.P. Farrell & S.P. Heyneman (Eds.), *Textbooks in the developing world: Economic and educational choices* (pp. 141–172) Washington, DC: World Bank.

Eisemon, T.O. (1988). *Benefiting from basic education, school quality and functional literacy in Kenya.* Elmsford, NY: Pergamon.

Elley, W.B. (1992). *How in the world do students read?* Hamburg, Germany: International Association for the Evaluation of Educational Achievement.

Elley, W.B. (1994). *The IEA study of reading literacy: Achievement and instruction in thirty-two school systems.* Oxford, England: Pergamon.

Farrell, J.P., & Heyneman, S.P. (Eds.). (1989). *Textbooks in the developing world: Economic and educational choices.* Washington, DC: World Bank.

Gopinathan, S. (1978). *A measure of reading: IEA survey of reading interests and habits.* Singapore: Institute of Education.

Greaney, V. (1980). Factors related to amount and type of leisure-time reading. *Reading Research Quarterly, 15,* 337–357.

Greaney, V. (1986). Parental influences on reading. *The Reading Teacher, 39,* 813–816.

Greaney, V. (1993a). *Reading achievement levels and reading habits of Indonesian pupils.* Unpublished paper. Washington, DC: World Bank.

Greaney, V. (1993b). World illiteracy. In F. Lehr & J. Osborn (Eds.), *Reading, language and literacy: Instruction for the twenty-first century* (pp. 217–238). Hillsdale, NJ: Erlbaum.

Greaney, V., Khandker, S., & Alam, M. (in preparation). *Bangladesh: Assessing basic learning skills.* Washington, DC: World Bank.

Greaney, V., & Neuman, S. (1990). The functions of reading: A cross-cultural perspective. *Reading Research Quarterly, 25,* 172–195.

Guthrie, J.T., & Greaney, V. (1991). Literacy acts. In R. Barr, M.L. Kamil, P. Mosenthal, & P.D. Pearson (Eds.), *Handbook of reading research: Volume II* (pp. 68–96). White Plains, NY: Longman.

Guthrie, J.T., & Siefert, M. (1984). *Measuring readership: Rationale and technique.* Paris: United Nations Educational, Scientific and Cultural Organization.

Hanushek, E.A. (1995). Interpreting recent research on schooling in developing countries. *The World Bank Research Observer, 10,* 227–246.

Harbison, R.W., & Hanushek, E.A. (1992). *Educational performance of the poor: Lessons from northeast Brazil.* New York: Oxford University Press.

Herz, B., Subbarao, K., Habib, M., & Rainey, L. (1991). *Letting girls learn: Promising approaches in primary and secondary education* (World Bank Discussion Paper No. 133). Washington, DC: World Bank.

Hess, R.D., & Holloway, S. (1984). Family and school as educational institutions. In R.D. Parke (Ed.), *The family* (pp. 179–222). Chicago, IL: University of Chicago Press.

Heyneman, S.P., & Loxley, W. (1983). The effect of primary school quality on achievement across twenty-nine high and low income countries. *American Journal of Sociology, 88,* 1162–1194.

Hobcraft, J.N. (1993). Women's education, child welfare and child survival: A review of the evidence. *Health Transition Review, 3,* 159–175.

Ingham, J. (1982). *Books and reading development: The Bradford Book Flood Experiment.* London: Heinemann.

International Labor Office. (1992). *World Labour Report, 1992.* Geneva: Author.

Kats, I., & Pacheo, E.M. (1992). The crisis and challenge of book publishing in Asia [Special issue]. *Solidarity,* 135–136.

Kellaghan, T., & Greaney, V. (1992). *Using examinations to improve education* (Technical Paper No. 165). Washington, DC: World Bank.

Kelly, M.J. (1991). *Education in a declining economy: The case of Zambia* (Economic Development Institute, Development Policy Case Series No. 8). Washington, DC: World Bank.

King, E., & Hill, M.A. (1993). *Women's education in developing countries—barriers, benefits and policies.* Baltimore, MD: Johns Hopkins University.

Kremer, M.R. (1995). Research on schooling: What we know and what we don't. A comment on Hanushek. *The World Bank Research Observer, 10,* 247–254.

Lau, L.J., Jamison, D.T., Liu, S.C., & Rivkin, S. (1993). Education and economic growth: Some cross-sectional evidence from Brazil. *Journal of Development Economics, 41,* 45–70.

Levinger, B. (1994). Nutrition, health and school performance. *The Forum for Advancing Basic Education and Literacy, 3,* 2–4.

Lockheed, M.E., Verspoor, A.M., & Associates. (1991). *Improving primary education in developing countries.* New York: Oxford University Press.

Lundberg, I., & Linnakyla, P. (1992). *Teaching reading around the world.* Hamburg, Germany: International Association for the Evaluation of Educational Achievement.

Mathur, H.M. (1993). Human development: The sociocultural context. *Development and Cooperation, 2,* 4–5.

New book law in Colombia. (1995). *Journal of Reading, 38,* 677.

Office for Standards in Education. (1994). *Secondary education in Korea.* London: Her Majesty's Stationery Office.

O'Grady, B. (1994). *Teaching communities to educate girls in Balochistan.* Washington, DC: Academy for Educational Development.

Osa, O. (1986). The young Nigerian youth literature. *Journal of Reading*, 30, 100–104.

Pattanyak, D.P. (1993). Language policy and national cohesion. In L. Limage (Ed.), *Language policy, literature, and culture* (pp. 49–54). Paris: United Nations Educational, Scientific and Cultural Organization.

Peddling death to the poor. (1994, June 4). *Economist*, 43.

Pfau, R.H. (1980). The comparative study of classroom behaviors. *Comparative Education Review*, 24, 400–414.

Philippines, The Congressional Commission on Education. (1993). *Basic Education Vol. 1 The education ladder, Book 2 Making education work*. Quezon City: Congressional Oversight Committee on Education.

Pollitt, E. (1990). *Malnutrition and infection in the classroom*. Paris: United Nations Educational, Scientific and Cultural Organization.

Postlethwaite, T.N., & Ross, K.N. (1992). *Effective schools in reading: Implications for educational planners*. Hamburg, Germany: International Association for the Evaluation of Educational Achievement.

Preston, S.H. (1985). Mortality and development revisited. *Population Bulletin of the United Nations*, 18, 34–40.

Problems in book distribution. (1994). *Asian-Pacific Book Development*, 24, 3–4.

Purves, A.C. (1973). *Literature education in ten countries: An empirical study* (International Studies in Evaluation, Vol. 2). Stockholm: Almquist & Wiksell.

Puryear, J.M. (1995). International education statistics and research: Status and problems. *International Journal of Educational Development*, 15, 79–91.

Ramadas, L. (1994). Women and literacy: A quest for justice. In Z. Morsy (Ed.), *The challenge of illiteracy: From reflection to action* (pp. 11–22). New York: Garland.

Robinson, W. (1995). *How much fifth class math and science do our prospective primary teachers know?* Unpublished paper. Peshawar, Pakistan: Primary Education Program Coordination Office.

Ross, K.N., & Postlethwaite, T.N. (1994). Differences among countries in school resources and achievement. In W.B. Elley (Ed.), *The IEA study of reading literacy: Achievement and instruction in thirty-two school systems* (pp. 123–148). Oxford, England: Pergamon.

Sandstrom, S. (1995). Educating girls: The most effective investment in the developing world. *Bank's World*, 14, 16–19.

Schultz, T.P. (1993). Public investment in women's schooling. *The Forum for Advancing Basic Education and Literacy*, 3, 9.

Schultz, T.W. (1971). *Investment in human capital*. New York: Free Press.

Siddiqi, F., & Patrinos, H. (1995). *Child labor: Issues, causes and interventions* (Human Resources Development and Operations Policy Working Paper No. 56). Washington, DC: World Bank.

Smith, C. (1994). Health and adult literacy in Nepal. *The Forum for Advancing Basic Education and Literacy*, 3, 11–13.

Sorensen, C.W. (1994). Success and education in Korea. *Comparative Education Review*, 38, 10–35.

Southgate, V., Arnold, H., & Johnson, S. (1981). *Extending beginning reading*. London: Heinemann.

Spiegel, D.L. (1981). *Reading for pleasure: Guidelines*. Newark, DE: International Reading Association.

Summers, L. (1994). *Investing in all the people: Educating women in developing countries* (Economic Development Institute Paper Series No. 45). Washington, DC: World Bank.

Sun, M.T., & Deng, B. (1995, February). *Teacher education in China: Progress, challenges and reforms*. Paper presented at World Bank Seminar, Washington, DC.

Thorndike, R.L. (1973). *Reading comprehension education in fifteen countries: An empirical study* (International Studies in Evaluation, Vol. 3). Stockholm: Almquist & Wiksell.

Torres, R.M. (1994). Latin America and EFA: Inadequate and slow? EFA 2000, 14, 2.

United Nations Development Program. (1994). *Human development report*, 1994. New York: Oxford University Press.

United Nations Educational, Scientific and Cultural Organization. (1990a). *Basic education and literacy: World statistical indicators*. Paris: Author.

United Nations Educational, Scientific and Cultural Organization. (1990b). *Compendium of statistics on illiteracy*. Paris: Author.

United Nations Educational, Scientific and Cultural Organization. (1993). *Trends and projections of enrollment by level of education, by age and by sex, 1960–2025*. Paris: Author.

United Nations Educational, Scientific and Cultural Organization. (1994). *Statistical Yearbook*, 1994. Paris: Author.

Wagner, D.A. (1991). Literacy: Developing the future. In *International Yearbook of Education*, 43. Paris: United Nations Educational, Scientific and Cultural Organization.

Weiner, M. (1991). *The child and the state in India*. Princeton, NJ: Princeton University Press.

Wolfensohn, J.D. (1995, September). *Women in the transformation of the 21st century*. Address to the 4th United Nations Conference on Women, Beijing.

World Bank. (1988). *Education in Sub-Saharan Africa: Policies for adjustment, revitalization, and expansion*. Washington, DC: Author.

World Bank. (1993). *World development report*. Washington, DC: Author.

World Bank. (1995a). *Leveling the playing field: Giving girls an equal chance for basic education—Three countries' efforts*. Washington, DC: Author.

World Bank. (1995b). *Nutrition and early childhood development: Into the year* 2020 (Human Resources Development and Operations Policy Dissemination Note No. 47). Washington, DC: Author.

World Bank. (1995c). *Priorities and strategies for education*. Washington, DC: Author.

World Bank. (1995d). *Social indicators of development*. Washington, DC: Author.

World Bank. (1995e). *World development report*. Washington, DC: Author.

Zymelman, M., & De Stefano, J. (1989). *Primary school teachers' salaries in Sub-Saharan Africa* (World Bank Discussion Paper No. 45). Washington, DC: World Bank.

2 Lifting Literacy Levels in Developing Countries: Some Implications from an IEA Study

Warwick B. Elley

THE INTERNATIONAL ASSOCIATION for the Evaluation of Educational Achievement (IEA) comprises leading educational research centers in more than 50 countries around the world. Each year, representatives of these research centers meet and plan international studies, which are designed to help educators and policymakers improve student learning in their respective school systems. Over the past 30 years, IEA has completed studies of reading, mathematics, science, writing, civics, foreign-language learning, preprimary education, classroom interactions, and computers in the school. The increasing size of the organization and the widespread use of its findings testify to the value that member countries see in its unique style of research. There is a growing belief that educators in each country have something to learn from one another, not only in discovering their students' relative achievement levels in various aspects of the school curriculum, but also in revealing the range and effectiveness of their diverse methods and policies.

The first IEA reading study was conducted in 1970 to 1971 in 15 countries (Thorndike, 1973). The second study was approved by the IEA Assembly in 1988 and carried out over the following four years, this time in 32 countries. This chapter reports a number of findings that emerged from this study, relevant to the concerns of developing countries.

The IEA Study of Reading Literacy collected data on 210,000 students and 10,000 teachers in 32 education systems scattered throughout all continents of the globe. In 1990 to 1991 representative samples of students in each country responded to standardized reading tests and completed questionnaires about their home and school circumstances. What can this mammoth study tell us about the factors that differentiate high-literate from low-literate countries? Why is it that in some school systems nearly every student acquires a high level of literacy in less than three years of primary school, whereas in other countries large numbers of students pass through the school system and emerge unable to read? Are the reasons to be found primarily in the teacher training, class size, instructional emphasis, length of the school year, provision of textbooks, time spent on reading, involvement of parents, building of libraries, or other factors? In this chapter I will attempt to elucidate some of the factors that differentiated high- from low-scoring countries in this study. The hope is that such clarification might inform current policies for raising literacy levels in poorer countries.

Differences in School Literacy Levels Among Countries

The IEA study assessed students' literacy at two grade levels, one where the majority of 9-year-olds were found (Population A) and one where the majority of 14-year-olds were found (Population B). Stratified random samples of students and their teachers were selected for inclusion in each country, and adequate samples were drawn in nearly every country. There were minor differences in average age and grade level, but these had only slight effects on the outcomes. (See Elley, 1992, for more details.)

The reading literacy tests used were prepared by IEA members collectively, pilot-tested in all countries, and carefully edited to minimize bias. The tests were administered under standard conditions, and the results converted to a common scale with a mean of 500 and standard deviation of 100 at each population level. The mean scores for each country on this common scale showed that Finland's students had the best results at both age levels and in most subtests. Their mean scores clustered around 560 to 570 in each of the subtests. Other high-scoring countries at both age levels were France, Sweden, and New Zealand; the United States and Italy had impressive results in Population A.

The high-achieving countries were all Western countries with relatively sound economies, long literacy traditions, and strong indicators of social and health development. Developing countries did not perform very well. At the 14-year-old level (Population B), the lowest scoring countries were Botswana (with a mean overall score of 330), Zimbabwe (372), Nigeria (401), Venezuela (417), Philippines (430), and Thailand (477). Each of these six countries also showed low economic and health indicators and made up the last six countries on a composite index of wealth, health, and adult literacy.

At the 9-year-old level (Population A), the lowest scoring countries were again chiefly developing countries—Venezuela (383), Indonesia (394), and Trinidad and Tobago (451). (The other African and Asian countries at Population B level did not participate at age 9.) The overall mean scores for all countries are given in Figures 1 and 2.

What do these differences in average scores between high- and low-scoring countries really mean? How can we capture the differences in terms of daily literacy tasks? Here are some typical findings from the study to put the discrepancies in another perspective.

- Finland's 14-year-olds had approximately 80% of the literacy items correct, on average; the mean level for Botswana was only 27%. At the 9-year-old level, Finland scored 78% correct; the mean for Venezuela was 36%. These are enormous differences in a national cross-section of students of comparable age.

- At the low end of each national distribution there were a number of students who scored below chance level. This is one crude indication of nonreading status. By this index, Finland had 1% nonreaders at Population A level; Venezuela and Indonesia had more than 30% nonreaders.

- On a question requiring students to fill in given names, date of birth, and five other simple details on a travel form, New Zealand 14-year-olds averaged 94% correct; Botswana managed only 34%.

Figure 1 1990–1991 IEA Reading Literacy: Population A—Total Achievement Scores

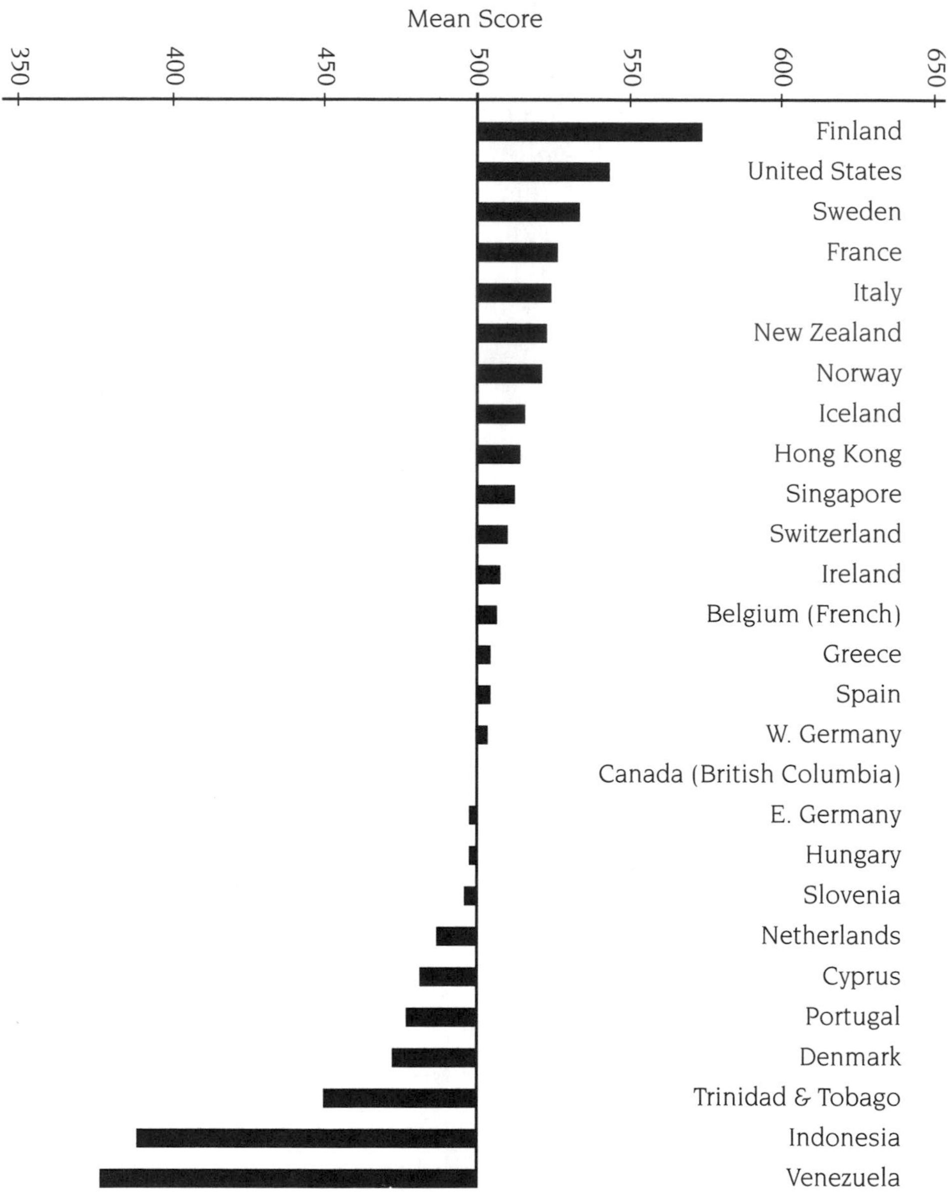

Mean Score

350	400	450	500	550	600	650	

Finland
United States
Sweden
France
Italy
New Zealand
Norway
Iceland
Hong Kong
Singapore
Switzerland
Ireland
Belgium (French)
Greece
Spain
W. Germany
Canada (British Columbia)
E. Germany
Hungary
Slovenia
Netherlands
Cyprus
Portugal
Denmark
Trinidad & Tobago
Indonesia
Venezuela

Figure 2   1990–1991 IEA Reading Literacy:
            Population B—Total Achievement Scores

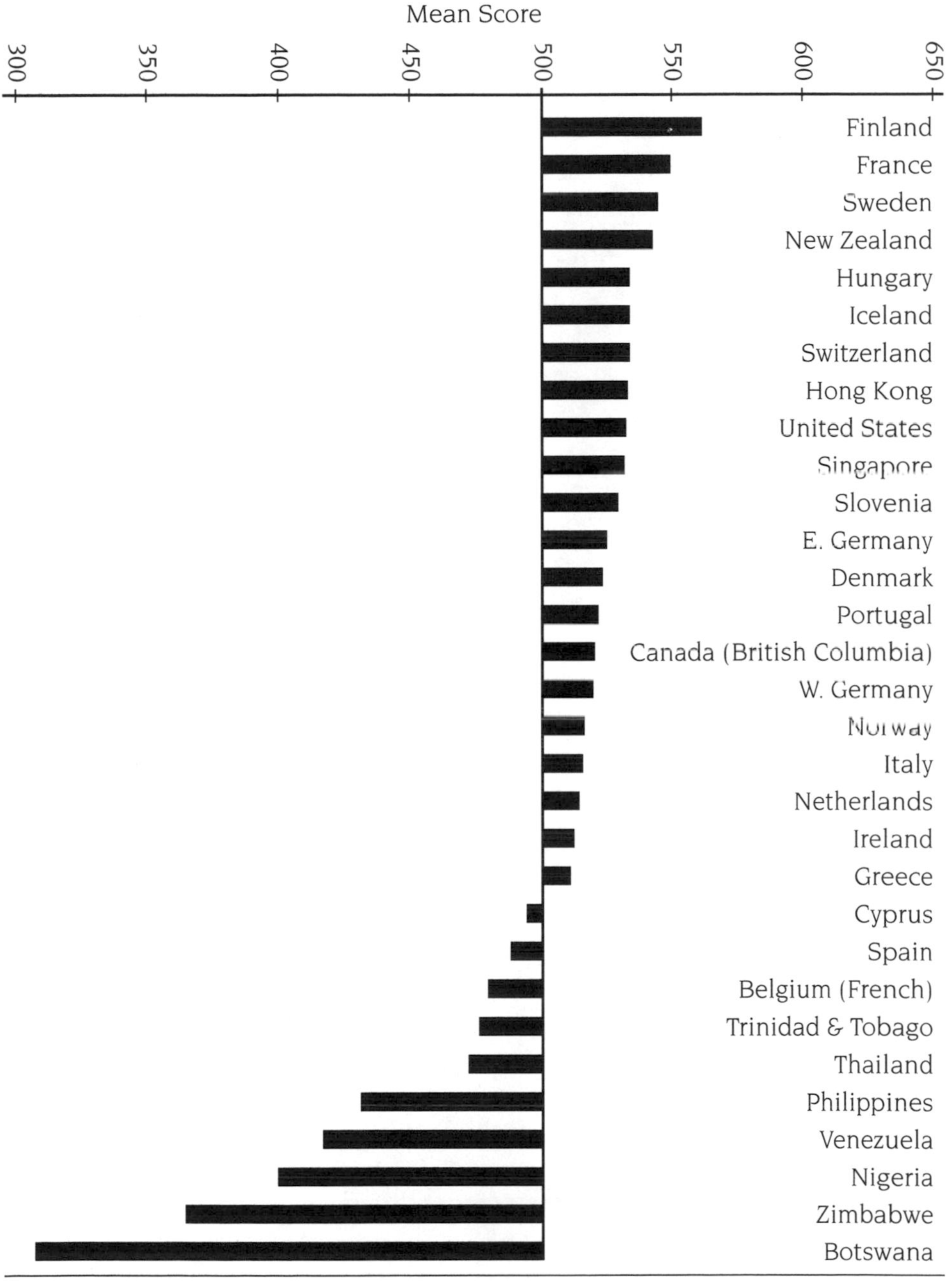

Mean Score

| 300 | 350 | 400 | 450 | 500 | 550 | 600 | 650 |

Finland
France
Sweden
New Zealand
Hungary
Iceland
Switzerland
Hong Kong
United States
Singapore
Slovenia
E. Germany
Denmark
Portugal
Canada (British Columbia)
W. Germany
Norway
Italy
Netherlands
Ireland
Greece
Cyprus
Spain
Belgium (French)
Trinidad & Tobago
Thailand
Philippines
Venezuela
Nigeria
Zimbabwe
Botswana

- On a question requiring students to read a bus timetable, French students averaged 87%; Nigerian students averaged only 33%.
- On a question about the advantages gained by an African woman who described her feelings when she became literate, Icelandic students averaged 84%; Venezuela managed only 25%.

Many more examples from the findings could be offered. The point is that although students in developed and developing countries are spending similar amounts of time in school, the outcomes of the education systems' efforts are clearly very different.

When evaluating education, it is best not to use enrollment statistics because they are grossly inadequate indicators of quality. More significant are such factors as the levels of funding, the education level of teachers, the quality of instruction, the support from homes, and the availability of reading materials. Thus, a report from the United Nations Educational, Scientific and Cultural Organization (UNESCO, 1991) points out that expenditure per student in 1991 in the developing countries of Africa, Asia, and Latin America was only US$93, compared with US$1,983 in the industrialized Western countries. Such figures translate into dramatic and disturbing contrasts in teaching conditions and quality of education. For instance, as Greaney mentioned in Chapter 1, in several African countries the average student-teacher ratio is more than 60; in Western Europe it is less than 20. The figures translate also into poorly trained and low-paid teachers, few books, inadequate buildings, unattractive classrooms, unsatisfactory seating, early dropouts, frequent failure, and low motivation for learning. In short, conditions that would cause a public outcry in industrialized countries are accepted as inevitable in developing countries. The resulting differences in educational outcome are obvious and understandable, but regrettable.

What Factors Are Most Highly Correlated with the National Differences in Literacy Levels?

It is obvious that the high-scoring countries have many advantages beyond the school. A Composite Development Index (CDI), made up of six indicators of wealth, health, and adult literacy (each with equal weight), showed a correlation of 0.70 to 0.80 with the national mean scores on the literacy tests. On the CDI scale, the high-scoring countries ranged from 4.2 to 3.1; the low-scoring countries ranged from 0.5 to 2.7. Clearly, students who are educated in a context where money is available to spend on schools and resources, students and teachers are relatively healthy, newspapers and other reading materials are readily available in the community, and most adults can read, will have an advantage. There is little doubt that adequate funds and the resources they purchase are important for quality education; no country in the study produced high literacy levels with low per-capita spending on schools. But money is not enough.

Table 1 lists a set of educational variables that often are claimed to be important in campaigns to raise achievement levels. (It is not a complete list of all the variables included in the IEA study.) The importance of each variable was calculated by comparing the 10 highest scoring countries with the 10 lowest (most of which were developing countries) and dividing the difference by the standard deviation for all countries. If, for any variable, there was little or no difference between the high- and low-scoring school systems, we could infer that this variable is not very important for raising literacy levels.

However, a straight comparison of this sort could be misleading. Sometimes a difference between high- and low-scoring countries may be merely a reflection of greater wealth. Consider class size, for instance. In Population B, the 10 highest scoring countries showed a mean class size of 24.2 students, and the lowest 10 countries showed a mean of 34.9. At first sight, one might conclude that small classes are better for improving literacy. However, small classes are also more commonly found in wealthy countries because maintaining a small student-teacher ratio is an expensive policy. To clarify the picture, the results were adjusted for CDI—in other words, we identified the 10 countries where students performed best, *relative to their* CDI, and compared their class sizes with the low-scoring group of countries. This time this low-scoring group contained both developing and developed countries. When this was done, the difference in class size disappeared. Countries in which students achieved the highest, relative to their CDI, had the same sized classes, on average, as those who achieved lowest. This suggests that class size is an indicator of wealth but not a good cross-national indicator of high-quality literacy education. Several countries (such as Hong Kong and Singapore) achieved very good results with typical classes of 30 to 40 students, whereas a few countries with smaller classes achieved below expectation.

Thus, using this stringent criterion, which of the many variables included in the IEA study showed the clearest differences between high- and low-scoring countries after adjustment for CDI? Which of these variables showed most promise for raising literacy levels in low-scoring countries? The results in Table 1 show the answers to these questions; only educational variables that are capable of ready manipulation in a country's policy are included in this analysis. (Further data are presented in Elley, 1992.)

Table 1 shows that at age 9, library size is an important variable in literacy achievement. The size of the school and classroom libraries differentiated clearly between education systems that produced high and low literacy scores, relative to the level of development of the society in which the students were educated. This finding is in line with

Table 1   Selected Variables That Differentiated Between High- and Low-Scoring Countries, Relative to CDI: Population A (Age 9)

Educational Variables	Effect Size*	Mean for High-Scoring Countries	Mean for Low-Scoring Countries
Large school library	0.82	3.50	2.06
Frequent silent reading	0.78	3.58	2.86
More instructional time (hrs)	0.60	22.80	19.70
Large classroom library (%)	0.51	55.10	43.50
More frequent reading tests	0.49	46.70	32.40
More female teachers (%)	0.40	78.40	71.80
More years teacher education	0.40	13.90	13.20
More library borrowing	0.31	3.06	2.90
More teacher reading to class	0.25	2.59	2.30
More textbooks per student	0.19	1.66	1.57

* Effect size was calculated by dividing the difference between the means of the high- and low-scoring 10 countries (relative to CDI) by the overall standard deviation.

Ready access to a wide range of books is a key factor in raising literacy levels. © Scott Walter
Used by permission.

similar large national surveys I have been involved with in Fiji (Elley
& Mangubhai, 1979) and in Indonesia (Mangindaan, Moegiadi, &
Livingstone, 1978; Moegiadi, Mangindaan, & Elley, 1979). Of course,
the quality and use of the library books are also important factors to
consider. In some developing countries the majority of the libraries'
contents may be textbooks, rather than fiction. Nevertheless, these figures confirm growing experimental evidence that ready access to a
wide range of books is a key factor in raising literacy levels (Elley,
1991). High reading scores are not found in countries that do not contain good school libraries.

The relative strength of the frequency of silent reading in class,
as reported by the teachers, is also apparent in Table 1. By contrast,
the number of language arts textbooks available to students, although
positive, was not significant in differentiating between high- and low-
scoring countries. However, this variable may be stronger in other
school subjects, such as mathematics or science.

Other variables in Table 1 that are directly relevant to the issue of regular reading by students are the apparent benefits of more instructional time, more library borrowing, more frequent reading tests, and more reading to the class by the teacher. (The last variable is not significant.) Although there are numerous other teacher characteristics that were thought to be potentially important (such as length of experience, native tongue, length of time with the class, and amount of personal reading), only the number of years of education and the gender of the teacher appeared in this cross-national analysis. The other characteristics varied between countries but did not correlate with achievement levels.

Table 2 shows that a similar pattern exists for Population B, as for Population A. Again, the low-scoring group included both developing and developed countries. At age 14, as at age 9, the level of school resources for literacy and the size of the school library are more important than the number of textbooks (which was surprisingly negative) or the frequency of testing. Other variables such as homework assigned, the gender of the teachers, and the level of teacher education

Table 2   Selected Variables That Differentiated Between High- and Low-Scoring Countries, Relative to CDI: Population B (Age 14)

Educational Variables	Effect Size*	Mean for High-Scoring Countries	Mean for Low-Scoring Countries
More female teachers (%)	1.35	76.40	51.10
More homework assignments	0.90	4.16	3.73
More school resources for reading	0.77	3.84	2.98
More years teacher education	0.63	15.60	14.72
Larger school library	0.53	4.20	2.70
More individual tuition (%)	0.42	52.50	44.50
More second-language students (%)	−0.38	10.00	19.90
More textbooks per student	−0.37	1.32	1.51
More reading comprehension tests	0.18	1.46	1.31
More frequent evaluation of teachers	−0.11	2.99	3.05
More instructional time (hrs)	−0.08	25.30	25.57

* Effect size was calculated by dividing the difference between the means of the high- and low-scoring 10 countries (relative to CDI) by the overall standard deviation.

are more significant at this age level, whereas the amount of instructional time is less important. One factor that had a predictable influence was the percentage of students whose first language was different from that of the test. Several low-scoring African countries had more than 50% of such students. Against this trend were low-scoring Venezuela (5.3%) and high-scoring Singapore (74.1%).

There were six low-income countries involved in Population B (Botswana, Nigeria, Philippines, Thailand, Venezuela, and Zimbabwe), and a further analysis was made of their figures for the 10 variables listed in Table 2. For most of these variables, there was little change in the conclusions, but the mean number of textbooks per student was found to be very low (only 1.0). Thus, a comparison with the top 10 high-scoring countries (adjusted for CDI) yielded a positive effect size of 0.63, whereas a straight comparison without adjustment showed an effect size of 0.32. These results are probably more realistic than those presented in Table 2, as the latter was affected by a few high-income countries with low achievement levels but many textbooks. Thus, the ratio of textbooks per student does correlate positively and significantly with national reading scores for Population B but still not as strongly as library size (which rose to 0.78). This conclusion is confirmed on Population A, with and without adjustment for CDI.

Which Should Take Precedence in Reading Instruction, Interest or Skills?

Another contrast between countries is worthy of attention. At both population levels teachers were asked to rate their aims in the teaching of reading. They were given 11 aims and asked to rank (from 1 to 5) the 5 aims to which they attached the highest priority in their instruction. Those aims for which there was a considerable contrast between countries are given in Table 3 for Population A and Table 4 for Population B.

Table 3 shows that teachers in high-scoring countries (adjusted for CDI) at Population A level gave much higher priority than teachers in low-income countries to aims concerned with interest and enjoyment of reading, whereas teachers in the five low-income countries in

Table 3   Mean of Teachers' Ranking of Selected Aims in Reading in High-Scoring and Low-Income Countries: Population A (Age 9)

Aim in Reading	10 High-Scoring Countries	5 Low-Income Countries	Effect Size
Develop a lasting interest in reading	3.10	2.26	1.05
Improve reading comprehension	3.10	2.58	0.81
Make reading enjoyable	1.93	1.28	0.77
Develop word attack skills	0.65	1.06	−0.91
Increase reading speed	0.30	0.62	−0.84

Table 4   Mean of Teachers' Ranking of Selected Aims in Reading in High-Scoring and Low-Income Countries: Population B (Age 14)

Aim in Reading	10 High-Scoring Countries	6 Low-Income Countries	Effect Size
Develop a lasting interest in reading	3.14	2.32	1.22
Develop critical thinking	2.43	2.05	0.66
Improve reading comprehension	2.33	2.70	−0.52
Extend vocabulary	1.63	1.95	−0.59
Increase reading speed	0.20	0.97	−2.20

Population A (Cyprus, Indonesia, Portugal, Trinidad and Tobago, and Venezuela) gave significantly more weight to skill development. The rating of interest development by teachers in Venezuela and Indonesia was very low.

A similar pattern was revealed in Population B (see Table 4). Teachers in high-scoring countries gave greatest weight to developing in students a lasting interest in reading. They were well ahead of teachers in the six low-income countries (for Population B, mentioned earlier) in this respect, who apparently viewed reading instruction more in terms of exercises in skill development. The students' achievement levels do little to endorse the validity of these priorities.

Such results are to be contrasted also with what students believe to be important in reading. The students in high-scoring countries were asked to select, from a list of 11 statements, which they thought represented the "best ways to become a good reader." In all countries, the most important factor selected was "liking to read," followed by "having lots of time to read." There may well be in this data an urgent message for teachers in low-income countries: creating in students a desire to read, to enjoy a good story, and to develop the habit of reading will be more beneficial than adhering to a regime that attempts to program students' growth by emphasizing systematic skill development.

It could be argued that the contrast in the teachers' values represents a responsible reaction to the students' present stage of development: where reading levels are low, teacher-directed skill development may be more important. To investigate this hypothesis, an analysis was made of the responses of the top 5% of readers in each country. On the IEA tests, these students were all competent readers and very similar across countries.

What do the best readers believe to be the best way to become a good reader? On 6 of the 11 ways provided, the good readers in the high-scoring countries showed a similar pattern of choice to the good readers in the low-scoring countries. But on five items, there were marked differences as indicated by their mean standard scores. In the high-scoring countries, the best readers selected "having many good books around" (with standard scores of +3.0 and −3.7 respectively for the high- and low-scoring countries), "having a lively imagination" (1.7 and −4.0), and "learning many new words" (2.3 and −3.2). In the low-scoring countries, by contrast, those three ways were unpopular with the good readers and were replaced by "learning how to sound out the words" (with standard scores of +5.9 and −4.9 respectively for the low- and high-scoring countries) and "doing drill at the hard things" (2.4 and −0.3). In other words, the good readers in the countries that have many nonreaders value skill teaching more than free-reading activities. Again these contrasting student ratings indicate that the programs that are most successful in keeping the proportion of nonreaders to a minimum are those that stress enjoyment of good books, rather than teacher-directed skills and drills. Successful reading programs appear to flourish in a context where many books are available and teachers encourage children to read and enjoy them.

What Are the Lessons for Developing Countries?

Cross-sectional studies rarely are able to generate clear-cut implications by themselves because the relations observed are only correlational, not causal. There may be other unmeasured explanations for the links observed. Nevertheless, the IEA Study of Reading Literacy was undertaken, and the questions to teachers were designed with clear hypotheses in mind, based on earlier experimental and cross-sectional evidence. A study of this kind has the potential to show the relative importance of book resources, time spent on reading, availability of textbooks, frequency of tests, teacher education, and other such modifiable variables. Many of these factors vary more between countries than they do within countries. Thus if they are important, their effects should be revealed more readily in an international study than they would be within a single nation. Likewise, if they are not of real consequence, a study design should confirm this fact. For example, size of school library and age of beginning instruction are two factors that are relatively homogeneous within countries but differ a great deal between countries. It takes an international study to reveal that the first is a strong correlate of reading achievement and the second is of minor significance.

With these qualifications and caveats in mind, it can be concluded that a key variable in raising literacy levels in the schools of developing countries is a ready supply of books, especially at the primary school level. The average school library contained more than 3,500 books in the developed countries that performed best (relative to their CDI); the average school library in the five low-income countries of Population A had about 600 books (and this figure was often inflated by including textbooks). There was a comparable distinct contrast in the classroom libraries. In the high-scoring countries more than 55% of primary school teachers reported having classroom libraries with more than 40 books; in the low-income countries, only 20.6% did. At Population B level, the high-scoring schools typically had libraries with more than 5,000 books, the low-scoring countries about 3,000 books. These discrepancies are in line with reading theories that claim that children learn to read primarily by reading—regular practice in an ability such as reading is required to develop competence. They are also in line with experimental research on the benefits of literature-based reading programs (Elley, 1991; Morrow, 1992).

Because children are doing progressively less reading in their leisure time and spending more time with television and computer games (Anderson, Wilson, & Fielding, 1988; Guthrie & Greaney, 1991), schools need to compensate for these trends by providing more opportunities to read at school. Another conclusion, drawn with reasonable confidence, is that instructional programs that stress teacher-directed drills and skills are less beneficial in raising literacy levels than programs that try to capture students' interest and encourage them to read independently. Where teachers allowed time for silent reading and encouraged children to read often, achievement levels were higher. This conclusion implies some reordering of priorities; inservice programs that introduce teachers to the potential value of good stories often have achieved this aim quickly with classroom teachers.

What Have We Learned?

There are more potential insights to be investigated in the IEA Study of Reading Literacy data. However, enough has been presented to suggest that the difference in school literacy levels between developed and developing nations is substantial and that much of this difference is attributable to a dearth of reading resources and literacy traditions in developing countries. As mentioned, education systems could do much more by supplying large quantities of suitable library books to schools and by developing programs that encourage students to read books often and enjoy them. These are simpler and faster prescriptions for lifting literacy levels than those that depend on extensive teacher education, principal training, or reduction in class size.

However, teachers are often reluctant to change from a traditional skills-based approach to reading instruction. It is worth noting that many teachers in Singapore were skeptical of the literature-based Reading and English Acquisition Program introduced into their highly structured primary programs by the Ministry of Education in 1985. Within weeks, however, most teachers were impressed by the new-found enthusiasm children had for reading and the rapid progress they made in their achievement (see Ng, 1987, and Elley, 1991; see also the section "The Influence of Book Floods" in Chapter 3 in this volume). The evaluations of this project and the high performance shown by Singapore children in the 1992 IEA Reading Literacy Study (see Figures 1 and 2 earlier in this chapter) are positive indications that literature-based programs are effective in Singapore schools. Similar observations were made about the literature-based programs introduced into Fiji primary schools, and the empirical comparisons left no doubt about the benefits of the large influx of books they received (see Chapter 8). Once teachers see the benefits of a literature-based approach in children's positive attitudes and higher achievement, they may be more willing to adopt this approach.

References

Anderson, R.C., Wilson, P.T., & Fielding, L.G. (1988). Growth in reading and how children spend their time outside of school. *Reading Research Quarterly*, 23, 285–303.

Elley, W.B. (1991). Acquiring literacy in a second language: The effect of book-based programs. *Language Learning*, 41, 375–411.

Elley, W.B. (1992). *How in the world do students read?* Hamburg, Germany: International Association for the Evaluation of Educational Achievement.

Elley, W.B., & Mangubhai, F. (1979). A research report on reading in Fiji. *Fiji English Teachers Journal*, 15, 1–7.

Guthrie, J.T., & Greaney, V. (1991). Literacy acts. In R. Barr, M.L. Kamil, P. Mosenthal, & P.D. Pearson (Eds.), *Handbook of reading research: Volume II* (pp. 68–96). White Plains, NY: Longman.

Mangindaan, C., Moegiadi, & Livingstone, I. (1978). *National assessment of the quality of Indonesian education: Survey of achievement in grade 9*. Indonesia: Ministry of Education and Culture.

Moegiadi, Mangindaan, C., & Elley, W.B. (1979). Evaluation of achievement in the Indonesian education system. *Evaluation in Education*, 2, 281–352.

Morrow, L.M. (1992). The impact of a literature-based program on literacy achievement, use of literature and attitudes of children from minority backgrounds. *Reading Research Quarterly*, 27, 250–275.

Ng, S.M. (1987). *Annual report on the reading and English acquisition programme*. Singapore: Ministry of Education.

Thorndike, R.L. (1973). *Reading comprehension education in fifteen countries: An empirical study* (International Studies in Evaluation, Vol. 3). Stockholm: Almquist & Wiksell.

United Nations Educational, Scientific and Cultural Organization. (1991). *World education report 1991*. Paris: Author.

3 | Research Foundations to Support Wide Reading

Richard C. Anderson

IN CHAPTERS 1 AND 2, Greaney and Elley emphasize that an increased supply of books to promote reading is necessary to raise literacy levels in developing countries. In this chapter I will review the evidence now available on whether literature-based instruction and wide reading actually have a positive influence on children's growth as readers. I will consider several areas of research: (1) vocabulary acquisition while reading as compared to direct vocabulary instruction, (2) the relation between amount of reading and growth in reading competence, (3) the influence of book floods, (4) the effects of whole language, and (5) available evidence on wide reading and literature-based instruction in the non-English-speaking developing world.

This review will focus primarily on empirical studies that have included measures of word recognition, basic comprehension of simple passages, and, especially, knowledge of word meanings. Although these facets of reading do not directly reflect the major goals of many advocates of literature-based instruction and wide reading, it is well established that measures of word recognition, passage comprehension, and vocabulary are powerful predictors of most aspects of literate behavior. As compared to children who perform well on these measures, children who perform poorly also will perform less well on almost any other measure of literacy; and it is a distressing fact that they are likely to continue to do poorly. Therefore, it is important to determine whether literature-based instruction and wide reading lead to improvements in basic literacy.

Literature-based instruction and wide reading often are placed in opposition to direct instruction on specific aspects of literacy. It seems necessary to say, therefore, that I do not suppose that a finding in favor of literature-based instruction and wide reading would count against direct instruction. Except in extreme cases, in which direct instruction in specific skills is the predominate or even exclusive form of instruction, such a conclusion would be neither logical nor empirically supportable.

Vocabulary Acquisition While Reading as Compared to Direct Vocabulary Instruction

Do children learn new words mostly from vocabulary instruction in school or from reading and other uses of language? This is a question that my colleagues William Nagy and Patricia Herman and I spent 10 years trying to answer. We believe we reached a conclusion which in its general outline is no longer open to dispute. Figure 1 presents a partial model of vocabulary acquisition; I will attempt to evaluate which of the paths in the model are most important for vocabulary acquisition.

Establishing Students' Vocabulary Size

The first questions that must be answered are how many words do students know and how many new words do they learn each year. If the average 12th grader knows 8,000 words, as some investigators have concluded (Dupuy, 1974), then it would seem that all a teacher would have to do is teach about 20 words a week for 12 years to cover all of the words. But if the average 12th grader knows 40,000 words, as other researchers have estimated (Anderson & Freebody, 1981), a teacher would have to teach 20 words a day to cover all 40,000 words—a much more daunting task. If 12th graders know 40,000 words, it should be apparent that they did not learn many of them in vocabulary lessons.

As these figures suggest, estimates of vocabulary size have varied dramatically (Anderson & Freebody, 1981). The variation occurs because of differences in the procedures used by vocabulary researchers.

Figure 1   Partial Model of Vocabulary Growth

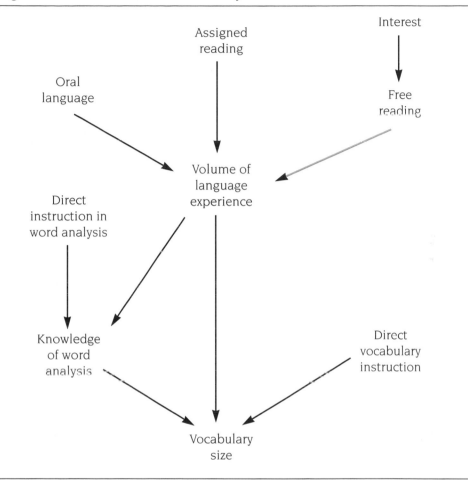

To estimate vocabulary size, researchers select a source of words, usually a dictionary, that is considered representative of English or some
other language; define criteria for selecting a sample of words from
this source; devise a test to assess knowledge of the sample of words;
give the test to a representative sample of children; and extrapolate
the results to all words and all children. Errors of estimation can arise
at any of these steps. For example, the size of estimates depends on
the word source: a researcher who selects words from a pocket dictio-

nary will conclude that the size of the vocabulary learning task is smaller than that estimated by a researcher who selects words from an unabridged dictionary.

Another reason for inconsistencies in the size of estimates comes from the definition of what is considered a distinct word in English. Everyone agrees that, for instance, <u>dog</u> and <u>dogs</u> or <u>look</u>, <u>looks</u>, <u>looked</u>, and <u>looking</u> should not be counted as separate words. Beyond simple inflections such as these, however, there has been continuing controversy about the proper definition of a functionally distinct word. Researchers who, for instance, group <u>carriage</u> with <u>carry</u> and <u>nevertheless</u> with <u>never</u> arrive at smaller estimates of vocabulary size than researchers who count these as distinct words.

Nagy and I (1984) attempted to resolve questions about the size of the vocabulary learning task. First, instead of using either a large or a small dictionary, we employed the Carroll, Davies, and Richman (1971) corpus of more than 5 million running words from a thousand items of published materials in use in schools. The materials sampled included textbooks, workbooks, kits, novels, general nonfiction, encyclopedias, and magazines chosen to represent, as nearly as possible, the range of required and recommended school reading.

We analyzed relatedness among words, not in terms of their historical derivations, as many before us have done, but in terms of the similarity of their current meanings. We judged pairs of words, attempting to decide whether a student who knew the meaning of only one of the words would be able to infer the meaning of the other word upon encountering it in context while reading. We judged, for example, that most students who knew <u>sweet</u> would be able to understand <u>sweetness</u>, but that knowing <u>busy</u> usually would be insufficient to understand <u>business</u>. Compound words were judged in a similar fashion. For example, with some help from context, most students could infer <u>foglights</u> if they knew <u>fog</u> and <u>light</u>, but knowing <u>fox</u> and <u>trot</u> would be little help to them in inducing the meaning of <u>foxtrot</u>, assuming they did not already know that compound word.

Based on an in-depth analysis of a 7,000 word sample from the Carroll, Davies, and Richman (1971) corpus, we calculated that there are about 88,500 distinct words in printed school English. Next we recalibrated previous estimates of the number of words known by students in different grades, using bench marks from our analysis (Nagy & Herman, 1987). When we applied the same definition of a distinct word in English, the variability in estimates of students' vocabulary size was substantially smaller. We concluded that the average 12th grader probably does know about 40,000 words and that the average student in primary or secondary school probably learns 2,000 to 3,000 new words each year.

We have decided that our previous estimate of 88,500 distinct words in printed school English is too small (Anderson & Nagy, 1992). It does not include any proper words, although writers are likely to assume the meanings of proper words such as <u>Moslem</u>, <u>Pacific</u>, or <u>Republican</u>. Nor does our previous estimate include multiple meanings of words, although knowing one meaning of a word is more likely to be a hindrance than a help in recognizing another meaning. For instance, knowing <u>bear</u> to mean a large animal does not help a reader understand <u>to bear a child</u>.

The largest category omitted from our previous estimate was idioms—any expression made up of two or more words, whose meaning is not fully predictable from the meanings of its parts. This definition covers a broad range of expressions beyond just colloquial expressions such as kick the <u>bucket</u>. It also covers stock phrases such as <u>by and large</u>; technical terms such as <u>standard deviation</u>; and ubiquitous compound verbs such as <u>put out</u> (as in <u>put out the fire</u>), <u>put up</u> (as in <u>put up the money</u>), and <u>put up with</u> (as in <u>put up with the noisy teenagers</u>). Most native speakers use and understand idioms without being fully aware of their frequency or the fact that their meanings are more than, or different from, the sum of their parts. <u>Make yourself at home</u> may sound like a regular, literal phrase, but <u>make yourself at house</u>, although presumably similar in meaning, does not sound like normal English. Moreover, some idioms, such as <u>by and large</u>, are not analyzable, because it is almost impossible to see any relation between the meanings of the component words and the meaning of the expression.

Derivatives and compounds whose meanings are distant from their roots, unknown proper words, unknown alternate meanings, and unknown idioms complicate the task of reading in the same way as unknown basic words. Thus, a complete assessment of the size of the vocabulary learning task would have to take account of these categories. There is limited research on how many derivatives, compounds, multiple meanings of homonyms, and idioms students know, but they certainly know thousands of items in these categories (see Anglin, 1993). Therefore, estimates of how many vocabulary items students of different ages know will have to be increased. Just how much must await further empirical research. In the meantime, we have guessed that, if an inclusive definition is used, there may be 180,000 distinct vocabulary items in school English, that an average 12th grader may know 80,000 of them, and that students may learn 4,000 to 6,000 new items each year (Anderson & Nagy, 1992).

Vocabulary Learning While Reading

Now that we have some idea of the size of the vocabulary learning task for English-speaking children, we can address the question of where and how they acquire the words they know. The first source I will consider is natural learning while reading—acquiring word meanings from context as the incidental byproduct of reading.

The idea that reading could play a major role in vocabulary acquisition has been attractive to many reading educators, dating back to Huey (1908) and Thorndike (1917), although early research failed to produce convincing evidence in favor of the idea (Gray & Holmes, 1938). Nagy, Herman, and I (1985) theorized that learning from context while reading is a gradual, incremental process. We argued that previous research had been inconclusive because the measures employed were insensitive to small increments in word knowledge and because the research designs were not powerful enough to detect small increments. Improved measurement and design has led to a different conclusion. Beginning with Jenkins, Stein, and Wysocki (1984) and Nagy, Herman, and Anderson (1985), a number of studies have now found reliable learning of word meanings from context during more or less normal reading (Herman et al., 1987; Nagy, Anderson, & Herman, 1987; Shefelbine, 1990; Shu, Anderson, & Zhang, 1995).

One study in which I was involved (Nagy, Anderson, & Herman, 1987) examined the word learning of 352 U.S. students in the third, fifth, and seventh grades. At each grade, four texts were selected from grade-level books. A random half of the students in each class read two of the texts, and half read the other two texts. Several days later all the students were tested on knowledge of the meanings of difficult target words from all the texts. The logic was that, if reading leads naturally to word learning, students who had read a text would perform better on a test of difficult words from the text than students who had not read the text. This design controlled for variation due to classroom climate; story difficulty and interest; and differences among the children in ability, motivation, and prior knowledge of the words, factors that might otherwise have overwhelmed the expected small influence of reading.

To increase sensitivity to partial knowledge, the vocabulary test we employed contained an easy and a difficult multiple-choice question for each target word. Question difficulty was manipulated by varying the similarity of the distracters (the incorrect multiple-choice answers) to the correct answer. The correct answer to the easy question was a synonym or in the general category of the target word. The distracters were definitions of words distant in meaning from the target word. Thus, a child who knew anything about the meaning of the target word had a good chance of selecting the correct answer. In contrast, the correct answer for the difficult question consisted of the exact definition of the target word, and the distracters included the definitions of words close in meaning to the target word. So, selecting the correct answer was not likely unless a child had more complete and discriminating knowledge of the target word.

We found small but highly reliable increments in word knowledge attributable to reading at all grades and ability levels. The overall likelihood of learning an unfamiliar word while reading was about 1 in 20. The likelihood ranged from better than 1 in 10 when children were reading easy narratives to near zero when they were reading difficult expositions.

At first glance, the likelihood of incidental learning of word meanings while reading may seem too small to be of any practical value. However, further reflection will show that one must consider how much reading children do to assess properly the contribution of reading to vocabulary growth.

How much does the average child read? According to Anderson, Wilson, and Fielding (1988), the average U.S. fifth grader reads about

600,000 words a year from books, magazines, and newspapers out-side of school. If a student reads 15 minutes a day in school, another 600,000 words of text could be covered. Thus, a conservative estimate of the total volume of reading of a typical U.S. fifth grader is 1 million or more words per year, although many children read two or three or even five times this amount.

How many new words do children acquire in a year simply from reading? We have estimated that a child who reads 1 million words a year will encounter at least 20,000 unfamiliar words. With a 5% chance of learning a word, it follows that the typical child may be learning about 1,000 words a year from reading. This is a low estimate: when reading self-selected material or assigned material that is not too dif-ficult, the chances of learning an unfamiliar word rise to 10% or more, and the yearly yield may be 2,000 words or as many as 4,000 if proper names, alternate meanings of homonyms, and idioms are considered. These figures represent the expected yield for children who do an

Increasing the amount of children's playful, stimulating experience with good books leads to accelerated growth in reading competence. © Pamela Winsor. Used by permission.

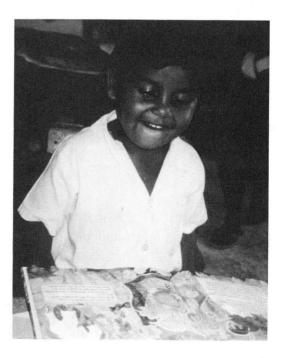

average amount of reading; avid readers may be learning two or three times as many words simply from reading.

Vocabulary Learning from Direct Instruction

How many words do children learn from direct vocabulary instruction in school each year? Nagy and Herman (1987) counted the number of words listed to be taught by several basal reading programs for third through sixth grade. The number ranged from 290 to 460. These were words "new" to the basal reading program, but studies show that students already can read and understand as many as 70% of them (Roser & Juel, 1982). Moreover, classroom observation suggests that the typical teacher skips most of the recommended vocabulary instruction (Durkin, 1979; Roser & Juel, 1982). Classroom observation also suggests that not much vocabulary instruction occurs during content area reading instruction (Durkin, 1979). Nagy and Herman (1987) surmised that in the typical classroom 300 words a year, at most, are covered in instruction aimed specifically at word learning.

Of course, not every word that is "covered" is learned. Rich, varied, and intensive vocabulary instruction may lead to a rate of learning as high as 67% or more (Beck, McKeown, & McCaslin, 1983). In contrast, when all students do is study definitions and compose sentences using the words, the average rate of learning is much lower, maybe as low as 33% or less (McKeown, 1993; Miller & Gildea, 1987).

Assuming that the typical student receives instruction in about 300 unfamiliar words each year, and that the typical rate of learning is 33%, vocabulary instruction would result in the learning of 100 new words a year. With superior instruction, the rate of learning might rise to 67% and the annual gain to 200 words. The number could be considerably higher than 200 in classrooms where substantial time and effort are devoted to vocabulary instruction. Nonetheless, as Nagy and Herman (1987) have concluded, even in an ideal program of vocabulary instruction, the number of words actually learned in a year will still be in the hundreds. In contrast, the number of words learned in a year from independent reading is in the thousands for the typical child. So, regardless of whether conservative or liberal assumptions are made, independent reading appears to be a far more important source of vocabulary growth than direct vocabulary instruction.

Vocabulary Growth from Using Oral Language

Looking again at Figure 1, next I will consider the role of oral language in vocabulary growth. Oral language is primary for young children, and it continues to be important for all kinds of learning throughout life. However, there is good reason to doubt that oral language is the primary source for vocabulary growth when a child has become a fluent and frequent reader. This is because conversations and popular television shows do not contain a sufficiently rich vocabulary to allow for much growth. According to Hayes (1988, p. 584), a leading authority on vocabulary,

> Daily newspapers, most popular magazines, and even most comic books contain several times as many rare terms as conversation and television. While some sections of the newspaper are avoided by children, the comics, sports, Ann Landers–like columns, and the entertainment sections all provide at least twice as many rare words per thousand as natural conversation. Children's books such as *The Black Stallion* or the Nancy Drew series are on average three times richer in these terms than texts of comparable length from parent or teacher speech. Books designed to be read to preschool children have texts whose lexical pitch is 50% higher than average adult-child talk. Even Peter Rabbit and the Bugs Bunny cartoons are expressed at two or three times higher a lexical pitch than adult-child talk.

A special case of oral language is reading aloud to children. When there is discussion of a book, as in the shared book approach (Holdaway, 1979), there is direct evidence of increased word learning (Elley, 1991; Feitelson, Kita, & Goldstein, 1986). Captioning a television program is another enhancement of oral language that increases word learning (Neuman & Koskinen, 1992). Further, words that are partly known from oral language are more likely to be learned when encountered during independent reading (Nagy, Anderson, & Herman, 1987; Shu, Anderson, & Zhang, 1995).

In conclusion, the best available evidence suggests that at least one-third, and maybe as much as two-thirds, of the typical child's annual vocabulary growth comes as the natural consequence of reading books, magazines, and newspapers. It appears that reading may be about 10 times as important a source of vocabulary growth as direct vocabulary instruction. Although the exact contribution of oral language to vocabulary growth cannot be delimited at this time, there is reason to believe that, once a child has learned to read, reading is a more important direct source of word learning than oral language.

Amount of Reading and Growth in Reading Competence

How much does the average child read? How extensive is the variation among children in amount of reading? Is variation in amount of reading associated with rate of growth in reading proficiency? Numerous studies of children's reading habits have been completed, but there are serious faults with the majority of them. A characteristic fault has been overreliance on questionnaires to assess amount of reading. It is not easy to have confidence in an assessment that requires children to remember their activities over lengthy periods of time, to discriminate precisely between options such as "usually" and "often," or to refrain from circling the socially desirable larger number instead of the possibly more accurate smaller number.

Among the studies using sound methods is one conducted by Greaney (1980) in Ireland. Nearly 1,000 fifth-grade students from 31 Irish primary schools completed diaries of out-of-school activities for several days. Analysis of the diary entries revealed wide individual variation in amount of reading. Fully 44% of the students did not read books on any of the three days they completed diaries, whereas 6.4% devoted at least an hour a day of their leisure time to book reading. Greaney reported a positive correlation between book reading time and a standardized measure of reading achievement.

Colleagues and I (Anderson, Wilson, & Fielding, 1988) performed a study similar to Greaney's in the United States. A total of 155 fifth-grade students from two schools completed activity diaries recording out-of-school activities for periods ranging from 8 to 26 weeks. Every morning the students wrote on a form how many minutes they spent the previous day on each activity. Table 1 reproduces the principal findings of the study. The scale is percentile rank on each of several measures of amount of reading.

The table shows profound differences among children in amount of reading. Starting at the bottom of the table, notice that successive

Table 1   Variation in Amount of Independent Reading

Percentile Rank[a]	Minutes of Reading per Day		Words Read per Year	
	Books	Text[b]	Books	Text[b]
98	65.0	67.3	4,358,000	4,733,000
90	21.2	33.4	1,823,000	2,357,000
80	14.2	24.6	1,146,000	1,697,000
70	9.6	16.9	622,000	1,168,000
60	6.5	13.1	432,000	722,000
50	4.6	9.2	282,000	601,000
40	3.2	6.2	200,000	421,000
30	1.8	4.3	106,000	251,000
20	.7	2.4	21,000	134,000
10	.1	1.0	8,000	51,000
2	0	0	0	8,000

[a] Percentile rank on each measure separately.
[b] Books, magazines, and newspapers.
Adapted from "Growth in Reading and How Children Spend Their Time Outside of School," by R.C. Anderson, P.T. Wilson, and L.G. Fielding, 1988, *Reading Research Quarterly*, 23, p. 292.

groups of children read for increasingly long periods of time and covered increasingly large numbers of words. For example, the child who was at the 90th percentile in amount of book reading spent nearly 5 times as many minutes per day reading books as the child at the 50th percentile and more than 200 times as many minutes per day reading books as the child at the 10th percentile.

Notice, also, that the average fifth grader in this study was not reading very much. Table 1 shows that the median child read books for a little less than 5 minutes per day and only read 9 minutes a day when magazines and newspapers are considered in addition to books. Other research confirms that children in the United States do not read very much (Allen, Cipielewski, & Stanovich, 1992; Walberg & Tsai, 1984).

We (Anderson, Wilson, & Fielding, 1988) found significant, positive relation between the measures of amount of reading, particularly amount of book reading, and measures of reading comprehension, vocabulary, and reading speed. Perhaps most interesting and important was that the number of minutes a day reading books was a significant predictor of growth in reading proficiency between the second and the fifth grade, after statistically controlling for second-grade reading level. This suggests that reading books may be a *cause*, not merely a *reflection*, of children's level of reading proficiency.

A series of studies by Stanovich and his associates (Stanovich, 1993) has added substantially to knowledge about the relation between amount of reading and reading proficiency. These studies employ several measures of amount of reading. One is an author recognition test: students check the authors of children's books on a list of peoples' names; to catch the student who is just guessing, some of the names on the list are not authors of children's books. Another measure, the title recognition test, requires students to pick the titles of books from among a list of possible titles, some of which are not really book titles. Except for the fact they do not permit estimates of the absolute amount of reading, the two tests appear to measure amount of reading just as well as the activity diary method, but with much less time and trouble (Allen, Cipielewski, & Stanovich, 1992).

Using the author and title recognition tests, Stanovich and his collaborators have confirmed the results of Anderson, Wilson, and Fielding (1988), finding that amount of reading is significantly associated with growth in reading comprehension between third grade and fifth or sixth grade, after statistically controlling for third-grade reading level (Cipielewski & Stanovich, 1992). In other studies with adults as well as children, they have found that amount of reading is strongly associated with vocabulary knowledge, verbal fluency, spelling, general information, knowledge of history and literature, and cultural literacy, after statistically controlling for such factors as decoding skill, nonverbal intelligence, and age (Cunningham & Stanovich, 1991; Stanovich & Cunningham, 1992).

In a naturalistic study, West, Stanovich, and Mitchell (1993) unobtrusively observed travelers in departure lounges at National Airport in Washington, DC. A person under observation was classified as a "reader" if he or she read for 10 consecutive minutes and a "nonreader" if he or she read nothing during the 10-minute observation period. A total of 217 people classified in this manner were approached and agreed to take a battery of tests. The results are displayed in Table 2. Readers performed significantly better than nonreaders on all the measures, except the ones involving television. On each measure, the

Table 2   Mean Scores of Readers and Nonreaders at Washington, DC
National Airport

Variable	Readers	Nonreaders	*t* Test
Author recognition test	.635	.401	7.75*
Magazine recognition test	.751	.598	5.21*
Newspaper recognition test	.529	.370	6.12*
Television programs checklist	.352	.366	−0.51
Television newsperson names	.650	.578	3.37*
Television characters and actors	.392	.363	1.06
Film recognition test	.320	.292	1.10
Vocabulary checklist	.731	.516	7.57*
Cultural literacy test	.770	.600	7.00*

*$p < .01$
Adapted from "Reading in the Real World and Its Correlates," by R.F. West, K.E. Stanovich, and
H. Mitchell, 1993, *Reading Research Quarterly*, 28, p. 40.

advantage remained significant after statistically removing the influence due to age and years of education.

The conclusion from the studies reviewed in this section is that amount of reading is consistently associated with an array of indicators of reading proficiency and topical knowledge. Studies of natural variation in reading are necessarily correlational, so these studies fall short of proving that amount of reading causes these effects. Still, several of the studies have included controls for earlier reading level, basic decoding skill, nonverbal intelligence, age, or years of education. Therefore, it seems safe to conclude, at least, that amount of reading is strongly implicated as a major factor in growth in literacy.

The Influence of Book Floods

The best way to establish whether amount of reading influences growth in reading proficiency would be to evaluate interventions that demonstrably increase the amount of reading that children do. This has been done in research by Elley, Watson, and Cowie (1976). In nine studies in the South Pacific and Southeast Asia, they have evaluated book floods and associated practices with children learning English as a second language. (See also Chapter 8 by Elley in this volume.)

As the name given to the intervention "book flood" implies, students were immersed in appealing books designed to be read, discussed, and shared in various ways. The books were written to interest children, and they ranged widely in difficulty without tight control over vocabulary or syntax. Books were read often to younger children by the teacher, using a shared book approach (Holdaway, 1979). Older children usually read the books independently.

All nine of the studies show large benefits from book floods. Research on the Reading and English Acquisition Program (REAP) in Singapore, for example, documents higher scores on various measures by the children involved. REAP was introduced in 1985 at the 6-year-old level in 30 schools and systematically expanded over three years to 132 schools in 1987. This program included a range of books purchased by the Ministry of Education: 60 books per classroom to be used in shared book reading by the teacher and children, and another 150 to 200 books for independent reading by the children. Teachers received four to six workshop sessions supplemented with classroom visits. The non-REAP comparison program involved an audiolingual approach, which featured structured lessons designed to teach new vocabulary and syntactic forms systematically and to provide ample practice through oral and written exercises. Two of the three studies of REAP done in its final year are summarized in Table 3. In both studies (and in the third study) children who had been involved in REAP did much better on most measures.

There also has been research on book floods that involved children reading in their first language. Among these are a study in New Zealand (Elley, Watson, & Cowie, 1976), one in England (Ingham, 1982), and an unpublished study in the United States that my colleagues and I have done. The results of book floods with first-language learners have been positive but not as strong as the results of studies with second-language learners.

It should be noted that not all in-school programs intended to increase amount of reading lead to gains on tests of reading proficiency. Gains are more likely when the program endures a year or more (Krashen, 1993) and when book discussions are featured (Guthrie et al., 1995; Manning & Manning, 1984).

Table 3 Reading and English Acquisition Program in Singapore: Comparison of REAP and Non-REAP Mean Scores (Final Year)

	REAP Students	Non-REAP Students	t Test
Sample of 512 Students **(256 REAP and 256 non-REAP)**			
Burt Word Recognition Test	44.8	43.0	1.7
Record of Oral Language	18.1	17.3	1.0
Neale Analysis of Reading			
Accuracy	71.3	66.8	2.1*
Comprehension	21.8	18.9	3.8*
Retell a story	24.7	20.2	4.3**
Vocabulary	19.0	17.5	3.7**
Grammar	21.8	20.2	3.7**
Reading comprehension	9.6	8.7	3.6**
Listening comprehension	11.0	10.5	2.5*
Dictation	4.0	3.9	0.5
Writing			
Content	15.8	14.8	2.4*
Organization	2.9	2.9	0.0
Grammar	12.0	10.7	3.5**
Spelling errors	−0.9	−1.1	3.1**
Punctuation	−1.0	−1.3	2.7**
Writing total	28.9	26.0	3.4**
Sample of 700 Students			
Vocabulary	17.5	15.7	5.2**
Grammar	20.0	18.7	3.1**
Reading comprehension	8.6	8.0	2.8**
Listening comprehension	10.3	9.4	4.2**
Dictation	3.3	4.6	−7.3**
Writing			
Content	15.1	12.5	7.0**
Organization	3.2	3.1	1.2
Grammar	11.0	8.9	6.6**
Spelling errors	−1.2	−1.2	0.0
Punctuation	−1.2	−1.4	2.5*
Writing total	26.8	21.9	6.6**

*$p < .05$; **$p < .01$
Adapted from "Acquiring Literacy in a Second Language: The Effects of Book-Based Programs," by W.B. Elley, 1991, *Language Learning*, 41, p. 395.

Effects of Whole Language

Frequently, in the United States and in much of the rest of the English-speaking world, school programs intended to extend children's reading are labeled as "whole language" programs. Whole language is a total philosophy of literacy education, with sociopolitical assumptions as well as assumptions about instructional methods. Educators who believe in whole language have created much of the interest in wide reading, literature-based instruction, and integrated language arts.

Research on whole language has been inconclusive. Based on a meta-analysis of the United States Office of Education first-grade studies and of 46 additional studies, Stahl and Miller (1989) concluded that "overall, whole language/language experience approaches and basal reader approaches are approximately equal in their effects" (p. 87). The Stahl and Miller synthesis has been criticized for lumping whole language and language experience together, focusing narrowly on word identification and basic comprehension, and missing or undervaluing new research. Stahl, McKenna, and Pagnucco (1993) have attempted to accommodate these criticisms in a review of 45 studies that have appeared since the Stahl and Miller synthesis. However, the conclusions did not change very much between the two reviews. Both reviews found positive effects of whole language in kindergarten or whenever children first receive literacy instruction. Although the earlier review found slightly negative effects of whole language after kindergarten on word identification and basic comprehension, the trend in recent studies is toward slightly positive effects on measures of these competencies but no difference on measures of writing, orientation toward reading, or attitude. Stahl, McKenna, and Pagnucco also noted that effects are variable from study to study: for example, on measures of comprehension, effect sizes in recent studies vary from $-.74$ to $+1.63$.

Whole language theorists have responded to the inconsistencies in research purporting to evaluate whole language in several ways. They have argued that among the goals of whole language, effectiveness in promoting basic literacy is not very important, that the various tests and experiments disempower teachers, and that the whole language paradigm is incommensurate with the paradigm of those who have conducted comparative studies (Edelsky, 1990; Goodman,

1989). These responses may be missing a simpler point: the apparently weak and inconsistent results may mean that whole language has dysfunctional aspects or that the philosophy is being imperfectly realized in practice. Immersing children in literature is one of the axioms of whole language. The research I have reviewed elsewhere in this chapter shows fairly strong and rather consistent benefits to basic literacy from immersing children in literature. So, unless there are problems in the ways whole language is being realized in practice, it is otherwise curious why research has not been able to show consistent benefits in whole language classrooms.

Available Evidence on Literature-Based Instruction and Wide Reading in the Developing Non-English-Speaking World

Educational research studies in developing countries are neither plentiful nor easily accessible. Undoubtedly there are informative studies of which I am unaware; thus, I make no pretense about presenting a definitive review of relevant research. All I can say is that the studies in developing or non-English-speaking countries with which I am acquainted point to the same conclusions as the other research reviewed in this chapter.

Extending the research on vocabulary previously done only with English-speaking children, my colleagues and I (Shu, Anderson, & Zhang, 1995) completed a cross-cultural study of natural learning of word meanings while reading. A total of 447 Chinese and American children in third and fifth grades read one of two cross-translated stories and then completed a test on the difficult words in both stories. The results showed significant learning of word meanings while reading in both grades in both countries.

In the Chinese part of the study, amount of out-of-school reading was investigated at the beginning of the spring semester. We asked the children to write the names of books that they had read during the preceding winter vacation. The amount of out-of-school reading was coded as little (3 or fewer books), average (4 to 7 books), or much (8 or more books). Table 4 shows performance on a test of difficult words as a function of whether the children had read the text containing the words and amount of out-of-school reading. The column

Table 4   Learning of Unfamiliar Words by Chinese Third and Fifth
           Graders as a Function of Amount of Out-of-School Reading

Amount of Reading	Text Read	Text Not Read	Gain	Probability
Much	.76	.66	.10	.30
Average	.58	.54	.04	.09
Little	.49	.47	.02	.04

From "Incidental Learning of Word Meanings While Reading: A Chinese and American Cross-Cultural
Study," by H. Shu, R.C. Anderson, and H. Zhang, 1995, *Reading Research Quarterly*, 30, p. 89.

labeled "Text Not Read" presents the proportion of difficult words children knew without reading the text. This is a measure of preexisting vocabulary size, and it is apparent that children who read extensively
have larger vocabularies. The column labeled "Probability" indicates
the likelihood that the meaning of a previously unfamiliar word would
be acquired simply from reading a text containing the word. As can
be seen, the likelihood of learning the meaning of a word for children
who did much reading was more than three times as great as for children who did some reading, and more than seven times as great as
for children who did little or no reading. It is evident that Chinese
children who read extensively outside of school have learned how to
learn unfamiliar words.

The Chinese data show benefits from wide reading; however, data
from Indonesia suggest negative consequences when circumstances
conspire to keep rates of reading low (Greaney, 1992). The frequency of
out-of-school reading among Indonesian students is low by international standards. One reason appears to be lack of access to books. Almost two out of three primary students surveyed did not have a reading textbook, or they shared one with other students. Only half of the
primary classrooms were reported as having a library, and the number of titles was low in classrooms that did have libraries. Although
almost all schools had a central library, site visits suggested that the
word "library" can be misleading: "In most instances, libraries viewed
amounted to little more than storerooms for old and current textbooks. Books that might be read for pleasure or general information
were conspicuous by their absence" (Greaney, 1992, p. 4). Greaney ar-

gues that another reason for the low rates of voluntary reading among Indonesian students is that teachers give high priority to the development of reading skills but pay little or no attention to making reading enjoyable, as Elley mentioned in the previous chapter. Also, Elley's Figure 1 in Chapter 2 shows that in the recent IEA Study of Reading Literacy, Indonesian students ranked 26th in total achievement scores among the students in 27 participating countries.

Available studies generally suggest that the supply of interesting reading material that is available to children and the value that is placed on such activities as reading aloud from interesting literature to children are associated with attainment in literacy. This conclusion applies to children from various language groups, including Latino children learning Spanish (Schon, Hopkins, & Davis, 1982), Israeli children learning Hebrew (Feitelson, Kita, & Goldstein, 1986), and Arab children learning Arabic (Feitelson et al., 1993). The conclusion seems to be true, especially, for less privileged children from these groups. Krashen (1989, 1993) has reviewed studies of first- and second-language learning from around the world and has concluded that the evidence generally supports the thesis that growth in literacy is primarily determined by amount of "comprehensible input."

Wide Reading and Literature-Based Instruction Do Lead to Improvements in Literacy

In summary, there is a rather strong case, a case based on hard facts, that increasing the amount of children's playful, stimulating experience with good books leads to accelerated growth in reading competence. This conclusion appears to be a universal of written language development, true not only of English-speaking children learning to read English, but also true of children from various language groups learning their home language, a second language from their own country, or a foreign language.

References
Allen, L., Cipielewski, J., & Stanovich, K.E. (1992). Multiple indicators of children's reading habits and attitudes: Construct validity and cognitive correlates. *Journal of Educational Psychology*, 84, 489–503.

Anderson, R.C., & Freebody, P. (1981). Vocabulary knowledge. In J.T. Guthrie (Ed.), *Comprehension and teaching: Research reviews* (pp. 77–117). Newark, DE: International Reading Association.

Anderson, R.C., & Nagy, W.E. (1992, Winter). The vocabulary conundrum. *American Educator*, 14–18, 44–46.

Anderson, R.C., Wilson, P.T., & Fielding, L.G. (1988). Growth in reading and how children spend their time outside of school. *Reading Research Quarterly, 23*, 285–303.

Anglin, J.M. (1993). Vocabulary development: A morphological analysis. *Monographs of the Society for Research in Child Development, 58* (10, Serial No. 238). Chicago, IL: The University of Chicago Press.

Beck, I., McKeown, M., & McCaslin, E. (1983). Vocabulary development: All contexts are not created equal. *Elementary School Journal, 83*, 177–181.

Carroll, J.B., Davies, P., & Richman, B. (1971). *Word frequency book*. Boston, MA: Houghton Mifflin.

Cipielewski, J., & Stanovich, K.E. (1992). Predicting growth in reading ability from children's exposure to print. *Journal of Experimental Child Psychology, 54*, 74–89.

Cunningham, A.E., & Stanovich, K.E. (1991). Tracking the unique effects of print exposure in children: Associations with vocabulary, general knowledge, and spelling. *Journal of Educational Psychology, 83*, 264–274.

Dupuy, H.P. (1974). *The rationale, development and standardization of a basic word vocabulary test* (DHEW Publication No. HRA 74–1334). Washington, DC: U.S. Government Printing Office.

Durkin, D. (1979). What classroom observations reveal about reading comprehension instruction. *Reading Research Quarterly, 14*, 481–533.

Edelsky, C. (1990, November). Whose agenda is this anyway? A response to McKenna, Robinson, and Miller. *Educational Researcher, 19*, 7–11.

Elley, W.B. (1991). Acquiring literacy in a second language: The effects of book-based programs. *Language Learning, 41*, 375–411.

Elley, W.B., Watson, J.E., & Cowie, C.R. (1976). *The impact of a book flood*. Wellington, New Zealand: New Zealand Council for Educational Research.

Feitelson, D., Goldstein, Z., Iraqi, J., & Share, D.L. (1993). Effects of listening to story reading on aspects of literacy acquisition in a diglossic situation. *Reading Research Quarterly, 28*, 70–79.

Feitelson, D., Kita, B., & Goldstein, Z. (1986). Effects of listening to series stories on first graders' comprehension and use of language. *Research in the Teaching of English, 20*, 339–356.

Goodman, K. (1989). Whole language research: Foundations and development. *Elementary School Journal, 90*, 207–221.

Gray, W., & Holmes, E. (1938). *The development of meaning vocabularies in reading*. Chicago, IL: The University of Chicago Press.

Greaney, V. (1980). Factors related to amount and type of leisure-time reading. *Reading Research Quarterly, 15*, 337–357.

Greaney, V. (1992). *Reading achievement levels and reading habits of Indonesian pupils*. Unpublished paper. Washington, DC: World Bank.

Guthrie, J.T., Schafer, W., Wang, Y.Y., & Afflerbach, P. (1995). Relationships of instruction to amount of reading: An exploration of social, cognitive, and instructional connections. *Reading Research Quarterly, 30*, 8–25.

Hayes, D.P. (1988). Speaking and writing: Distinct patterns of word choice. *Journal of Memory and Language, 27*, 572–585.

Herman, P.A., Anderson, R.C., Pearson, P.D., & Nagy, W.E. (1987). Incidental acquisition of word meanings from expositions with varied text features. *Reading Research Quarterly, 22*, 263–284.

Holdaway, D. (1979). *Foundations of literacy.* Sydney: Ashton Scholastic.

Huey, E.B. (1908). *The psychology and pedagogy of reading.* New York: Macmillan.

Ingham, J. (1982). *Books and reading development: The Bradford Book Flood Experiment.* London: Heinemann.

Jenkins, J., Stein, M., & Wysocki, K. (1984). Learning vocabulary through reading. *American Educational Research Journal, 21*, 767–788.

Krashen, S.D. (1989). We acquire vocabulary and spelling by reading: Additional evidence for the input hypothesis. *Modern Language Journal, 73*, 440–465.

Krashen, S.D. (1993). *The power of reading: Insights from the research.* Englewood, CO: Libraries Unlimited.

Manning, G.L., & Manning, M. (1984). What models of recreational reading make a difference? *Reading World, 23*, 375–380.

McKeown, M.G. (1993). Creating effective definitions for young word learners. *Reading Research Quarterly, 28*, 16–31.

Miller, G.A., & Gildea, P. (1987). How children learn words. *Scientific American, 257*(3), 94–99.

Nagy, W.E., & Anderson, R.C. (1984). How many words are there in printed school English? *Reading Research Quarterly, 19*, 304–330.

Nagy, W.E., Anderson, R.C., & Herman, P.A. (1987). Learning word meanings from context during normal reading. *American Educational Research Journal, 24*, 237–270.

Nagy, W.E., & Herman, P.A. (1987). Breadth and depth of vocabulary knowledge: Implications for acquisition and instruction. In M. McKeown & M. Curtis (Eds.), *The nature of vocabulary acquisition* (pp. 19–35). Hillsdale, NJ: Erlbaum.

Nagy, W.E., Herman, P.A., & Anderson, R.C. (1985). Learning words from context. *Reading Research Quarterly, 20*, 233–253.

Neuman, D.B., & Koskinen, P. (1992). Captioned television as comprehensible input: Effects of incidental word learning from context for language minority students. *Reading Research Quarterly, 27*, 95–109.

Roser, N., & Juel, C. (1982). Effects of vocabulary instruction on reading comprehension. In J. Niles & L. Harris (Eds.), *New inquiries in reading research and instruction* (Thirty-first Yearbook of the National Reading Conference, pp. 110–118). Rochester, NY: National Reading Conference.

Schon, I., Hopkins, K.D., & Davis, W.A. (1982). The effects of books in Spanish and free reading time on Hispanic students' reading abilities and attitudes. *National Association of Bilingual Education Journal, 7*, 13–20.

Shefelbine, J.L. (1990). Student factors related to variability in learning word meanings from context. *Journal of Reading Behavior*, 22, 71–97.

Shu, H., Anderson, R.C., & Zhang, H. (1995). Incidental learning of word meanings while reading: A Chinese and American cross-cultural study. *Reading Research Quarterly*, 30, 76–95.

Stahl, S.A., McKenna, M.C., & Pagnucco, J.R. (1993). *The effects of whole language instruction: An update and a reappraisal.* Paper presented at the National Reading Conference, Charleston, SC.

Stahl, S.A., & Miller, P.D. (1989). Whole language and language experience approaches for beginning reading: A quantitative research synthesis. *Review of Educational Research*, 59, 87–116.

Stanovich, K.E. (1993). Does reading make you smarter? Literacy and the development of verbal intelligence. In H. Reese (Ed.), *Advances in Child Development*, 24, 133–180.

Stanovich, K.E., & Cunningham, A.E. (1992). Studying the consequences of literacy within a literate society: The cognitive correlates of print exposure. *Memory and Cognition*, 20, 51–68.

Thorndike, E.L. (1917). Reading and reasoning. A study of mistakes in paragraph reading. *Journal of Educational Psychology*, 8, 323–332.

Walberg, H.J., & Tsai, S. (1984). Reading achievement and diminishing returns to time. *Journal of Educational Psychology*, 76, 442–451.

West, R.F., Stanovich, K.E., & Mitchell, H. (1993). Reading in the real world and its correlates. *Reading Research Quarterly*, 28, 34–51.

4 | Textbooks in Developing Countries

João Oliveira

TEXTBOOKS ARE USED widely in both developed and developing countries. All member countries of the Organization for Economic Cooperation and Development (OECD) have vigorous, sustained textbook policies to guarantee the availability of textbooks in primary and secondary schools. In the United Kingdom, such policies date to the mid-19th century, when the government decided to allocate resources to buy three books per student. In the United States, an estimated 85% of classroom time spent on instruction involves using textbooks (Anderson, 1984; State of Florida, 1993). In countries with a high literacy tradition, such as Russia, textbooks are considered an essential tool for schooling. Even during Russia's transition to a market economy, with its accompanying shortages in various necessary supplies, the government has continued to provide textbooks as a priority item. Although the Russian government lacks a solid infrastructure to produce books, it is exemplary in the extremes to which it has gone to provide textbooks to its citizens.

Many other governments stress the importance of textbooks and appear to attach great value to them. Textbooks usually are seen as essential to foster linguistic and political unity as well as important cultural and ideological messages and values. In some countries government interest is reflected in committees established to scrutinize textbook language, content, and orientation.

Textbooks also are highly valued, desired, and used by teachers because they help them deliver the curriculum. Often, textbooks are the only written materials available to teachers that concern the curriculum, its contents, and its methods. Textbooks, then, become indispensable to teachers, particularly in situations where teacher training, pedagogic assistance, and supervision are rare, as is typical in most of the developing world. Teachers also rely on textbooks in countries where students must pass examinations in order to continue studying.

Importance of Books

Early studies by Coleman and others (1966) in the United States pointed to the strong influence of socioeconomic background variables on achievement and raised doubts about the effects of schooling or instructional materials, including textbooks, on students. In a country such as the United States, positive background factors, including the availability of reading materials and literate parents, give young students advantages over their counterparts from developing countries, as Greaney mentioned in Chapter 1. Textbooks may not contribute as much to students' learning in an environment where parents foster educational values and provide stimulating reading materials. This is not to say that schools in developed countries do not use textbooks; most rely on textbooks as the primary means of instruction, and students use these books daily to prepare for classes, study in class or for exams, and do practical activities and exercises.

Existing evidence suggests that textbooks are more important to developing countries than to those that are developed. In developing countries, where more than 70% of the world's population lives, books and opportunities to read outside the classroom are minimal. The poorer the background, Heyneman and Loxley (1983) have shown, the greater the impact of textbooks and schools. Variations in instructional materials appear to be reliable predictors of student achievement. This finding may be explained by a much higher variance in the quantity and quality of school materials in low-income countries than in high-income countries (Farrell & Heyneman, 1989).

Schools can be much more effective in promoting reading than homes devoid of reading materials, even when classes are poorly equipped and only a small number of books are available. When textbooks are scarce, students spend most of their time copying from several shared texts and in the process manage to acquire some reading skills. Empirical data have shown that the learning effects of textbooks emerge even when there is one textbook of doubtful quality for every two or three students (Harbison & Hanushek 1992).

Book Shortages in Developing Countries

In spite of their known impact on achievement, textbooks are a rare commodity in most developing countries. One book per student of any subject is the exception, not the rule. In Latin America, even middle-income countries such as Brazil, Uruguay, and Venezuela have failed to maintain a regular supply of textbooks over the past 15 years. Mexico's government provides substantial book coverage for the first 6 years of schooling, but mostly in urban areas and only for some of the subjects taught. Chile has developed a conceptually effective textbook policy, but it is still in its early years. Elsewhere during the last 15 years, China has used aid money to provide textbooks for most of its students. Jordan also has started textbook provision with World Bank funds.

According to the United Nations Educational, Scientific and Cultural Organization (UNESCO, 1991), out of 93 countries 57 responding to a questionnaire, or roughly 60%, report a sufficient supply of books. Yet, the fact that countries such as Paraguay, Burkina Faso, and Colombia are included in this 60% suggests that the term "sufficient" is highly ambiguous. Another 12 countries reported less than 30% "coverage" of textbooks. Despite these reports, the data suggest that access to textbooks is still very limited in the majority of developing countries, especially compared to the situation in OECD countries, where books tend to be available for all subject areas.

Textbook shortage data from other sources, such as the Executive Secretariat for the Andres-Bello Agreement of Andean Pact Countries (SECAB) (Hauzer et al., 1993), are hardly more reliable because they come from the same sources as UNESCO's data does: the ministries of education in each country. (As Greaney mentioned in Chapter 1, it is difficult to obtain accurate data from various countries' ministries of education for numerous reasons.) However, the situation

In spite of their known impact on achievement, textbooks are a rare commodity in most developing countries. © Brigitte Duces. Used by permission.

shown by the SECAB data is not much better than that shown by the UNESCO report: an overall rate of 32% textbook coverage is reported for countries such as Chile, Colombia, Bolivia, Ecuador, Panama, Peru, and Venezuela. Even allowing for the ambiguity in the concept "textbook coverage," it is still clear that the book shortage is undeniable. The SECAB report also shows that about 76% of primary school students (to third grade) have one primary or language arts book, about 30% have a math book, and fewer than 10% have another book. For the fourth and fifth grades, these figures drop by 20%.

My observations in countries such as Brazil, Mexico, Paraguay, Uruguay, and Venezuela support this perception of low levels of textbook provision. Data gathered for various World Bank projects on the availability of textbooks in schools and the publishing capacity and government purchases of textbooks in countries including Colombia, Ecuador, and Guatemala present an even bleaker picture. Again the limited data available consistently point to a situation of scarcity and erratic provision.

Although textbooks seldom cost more than 1% of total education budgets, governments in developing countries rarely supply them regularly. Two separate World Bank reports on Africa and Asia (World Bank, 1991, 1993) and a review by Askerud (1993), which included countries in other areas, concluded that virtually no developing country has managed to establish a policy and the means to produce and provide textbooks on a sustainable basis. Relatively few countries have specific budget line items to acquire instructional materials. Even when they do, as is typical in Latin America, the funds are not adequately invested, which leads to erratic policies and irregular provision. Some countries attempt to provide textbooks using outside money from donors or lending institutions. In many cases, such projects are seen by donors as means to develop a textbook infrastructure. However, these projects are usually fragile and seldom lead to institutionalization (Askerud, 1993; Searle, 1985). (See also Chapter 9 in this volume about donated book programs.)

Reasons for Book Shortages

If countries value textbooks and if they are so important to improve educational achievement, why are textbooks in such short supply? The shortage of textbooks is associated primarily with economics and is due to the expansion of educational opportunities. Until the mid-1960s in most of the developing world, schooling was limited to a relatively small proportion of the population. For example, in some former colonies in Africa, schooling was mostly restricted to the children of the elite. Often textbooks were produced in other countries and exported to the few existing schools in developing countries. Those able to send their children to school also were able to afford textbooks. Curricula were more stable, and as a result textbooks could be used over several generations. The attempts to expand schooling inexorably led to a weaker financial basis to support education. This was further complicated by the economic crises that most developing countries underwent since the first oil crisis. These crises were particularly acute during the 1980s, when real gross domestic product decreased in many parts of Africa, Asia, and Latin America; in the case of education, this adversely affected nonsalary educational expenditures for such items as textbooks.

Other factors related to weak provision derive from the types of policy adopted—more government emphasis on producing, publishing, and printing books than on developing a viable and competitive private sector. Some difficulties are also related to problems of management and the use of textbooks as tools of political patronage. A review of almost all World Bank–sponsored projects in Africa and Asia (1991, 1993) concluded that by concentrating too much on direct government publishing and on issues of short-term provision, Bank-financed national projects may have slowed progress on the establishment of a stable textbook industry. In spite of a growing number of technical assistance programs and projects with specific focus on textbooks, there seems to have been little or no improvement in recent years. A similar conclusion was reached by Askerud (1993): after reviewing the scarce existing literature and data and visiting a number of countries and virtually all international donor agencies working in these areas, Askerud determined that eight years later the problems encountered by many book development projects were much the same as those in 1985. Those problems include the lack of long-term interventions, poor curriculum and manuscript development, and inadequate manufacturing and distribution systems. Instructional material must be seen as an important element of the wider goal of creating a society where all types of printed materials are produced and read.

Effective textbook policies require a framework that includes provision for a viable publishing sector and some stability in curriculum requirements. Effective policies also require a clear understanding of the role of textbooks: textbooks must be seen as essential tools for the learning process, not tools for political patronage or items that may be provided to schools depending on the preferences of politicians or decision makers. Once the political will is in place, an infrastructure for the financing, production, distribution, and storage of textbooks must be established. Without the consistency in publishing guaranteed by a government textbook policy, however, private industry likely will be unwilling to risk becoming involved in textbook publishing. And governments are not typically well suited to perform such jobs as publishing and distribution. Jordan's success in providing textbooks and taking steps toward developing a sustainable textbook publishing industry, mentioned earlier, merits study. It is important to be aware that the process of creating a publishing industry is gradual. According to Tony Read, Managing Director of International Book Development, infrastructure for textbook publishing takes up to 15 years to develop fully. A publishing infrastructure for the nontextbook sector takes much longer. (See also the next chapter, by Read, about local publishing capacity.)

Supplementary Reading Materials: Should They Replace Textbooks?

The ultimate goal of literacy is to enable individuals to construct meaning from text. Children acquire meaning through interacting with words, sentences, and texts of all kinds and through accessing background knowledge to make predictions about the meaning of new text. Access to a variety of books and other reading materials such as magazines and newspapers facilitates that process. Reading becomes not a translation of the meaning provided by the text, but a transaction between author and reader in which both contribute to meaning. As Anderson and others (Anderson, Armbruster, & Kantor, 1980) have shown, understanding develops much faster when children interact with texts relevant to their own life experiences.

When these issues are considered, both critics of textbooks and some proponents of supplementary reading materials and literature-based instructional approaches, such as book floods and individualized reading, have ample ammunition for criticizing textbooks, in particular, language textbooks. First, the material presented in textbooks is often artificial and irrelevant to the lives of young students. Frequently textbooks are written to fit an instructional intent and then artificially used to fulfill that intent. As a result, children fail to see any purpose behind what they are reading. Traditional reading approaches tend to be mechanical and devoid of purpose. Second, many textbooks attempt to teach phonics, grammar, vocabulary, or linguistic structures in isolation. Rules for decoding or strategies to unveil meaning often are presented without reference to a meaningful context.

In addition, textbooks often convey the ideology of the dominant class of society, complete with biases. This effect is magnified when students have access only to a single book, as is common in developing countries, and are exposed to just one side of some issues. Textbooks have been criticized, and in some cases censored or banished, for the presence, absence, or inadequate treatment of matters such as religion, scientific beliefs, and historical figures (Bates, 1993; DelFattore, 1992). As a result, textbooks have become disreputable in many countries. Attempts to control or improve the quality of textbooks through regulations or committees often have led to more harm than good (Tyson-Berstein, 1988), distorted the authors' original intentions, threatened the integrity of textbooks, or led to watered-down versions of facts and issues (Oliveira, 1994). For these reasons, critics argue that textbooks should be replaced by meaningful reading materials.

Even if these criticisms were absolutely correct, and many of the existing textbooks including language textbooks could be considered inadequate, would it be feasible for developing countries to replace them with an abundant supply of other reading materials such as trade books? Following is a review of the most critical aspects of this proposition.

Cost Factors

Although the literature-based instructional approach answers many of the valid criticisms of textbooks, this strategy is clearly too expensive for implementation in the developing world. If 100 books are required per 30 students, assuming a unit cost of US$5 (the typical cost of a sturdy supplemental reading book in countries such as Argentina, Uruguay, or Chile, for example), a country would need to spend US$500 per classroom or US$16 per student. This figure could be reduced to US$8 by using the books in double-shift schools in which some grades are taught in the morning and others in the afternoon, and further reduced to US$4 by using the books over two years. If the books were used more than three years, the annual cost per pupil could be reduced to approximately US$2.66. Not included in these calculations are the related costs of teacher training, supervision, and storage necessitated by the introduction of nontextbook approaches to reading.

Lack of Capability

Developing the infrastructure to publish supplementary books may be well beyond the capability of many developing countries. If developing a textbook publishing industry takes an estimated 15 years, a more diversified one that could supply library and trade books would take considerably longer: print quantities are necessarily smaller, markets are reduced, language problems add to the complexity, and lack of distribution channels makes procurement and distribution complex. (See Read's Chapter 5 on developing local publishing capacity.)

Teacher Training

The educational background and training of teachers in the developing world also is essential when considering the application of a literature-based instructional approach. In a typical OECD country, teachers usually require a college degree plus satisfactory completion of a certification process in order to qualify for a position. In developing countries, teachers ideally have two years of normal school with some teacher training. However, many teachers have not completed their secondary education. One reason for the lack of training in these countries is that teachers tend to be poorly paid; there is little incentive for the better educated to pursue a career in teaching. And, because inservice training is rare, teachers have little opportunity to advance their skills. Frequently, teacher command of subject matter is poor. A study carried out in northeast Brazil demonstrated a finding typical of many South American classrooms: teachers scored lower than students on a general, multidisciplinary exam (Harbison & Hanushek, 1992). This study also noted that the little that students learned was determined mainly by their use of textbooks. More to the point, the study strongly suggests that teachers in developing countries lack the skills necessary to successfully implement a literature-based instructional approach.

Language Factors

Like textbooks, supplementary or trade books do not overcome the problems associated with teaching in multiple languages, a common situation in many developing countries, which Greaney discussed in Chapter 1. Of 58 countries studied by UNESCO (1991), 30 countries have two languages of instruction, and 15 countries have more than three. Further, in many countries the language of instruction is not necessarily the language spoken at home (especially in Africa and some Latin American countries).

Local languages create many problems from the perspective of publishing. If the local language is the only spoken language, text-books or supplementary reading materials are very expensive to produce. To maintain literacy skills, tremendous investments are needed to produce reading material in a local language for adults. Clay (1993) illustrates how some Pacific island countries successfully deal with this issue, although it is difficult to make generalizations from this setting to a larger population. In larger countries the local language typically is used during the early years of education to familiarize children with the process of learning. After the second or third year of school, instruction is shifted to another language such as French, English, Spanish, or Russian. There is some evidence that this approach yields better results than teaching literacy directly in a foreign language. But here, too, the materials used to teach the local language frequently are designed to stress phonic patterns that will later be transferred to the language of instruction, usually after the second or third grade. The instructional purpose of the materials and books is so specific that it makes sense for them to be published as primers or textbooks. Few countries, if any, can make the investments needed to produce additional relevant reading materials.

Limited Book Supply

Perhaps the biggest obstacle to literacy using nontextbook reading materials alone is the limited supply of books in developing countries. A broad choice of genre and subjects is important to engage a range of students' interests. In practice, the use of supplementary reading materials in developing countries means students read foreign books, typically produced in developed countries and highly focused on fiction rather than on other genre that may be more relevant to the students' experiences.

Most of the success stories of using nontextbooks for instruction in developing countries illustrated in this volume are based on applications using English, with its specific linguistic characteristics and abundant publishing record. Even in a developed country like the United States, where many school systems have been progressively implementing literature-based approaches, teachers still continue to use systematic instruction, primers, and structured textbooks in conjunction with the supplementary and trade book experiments (Durkin, 1993).

Although the supplementary reading approach may provide students with relevant materials, it is not free from some conceptual and practical limitations that are unlikely to be overcome soon in the majority of developing countries. Clearly, the ideal situation would be a combination of excellent teachers (and teaching guidelines) with abundant and varied reading materials for students. Developing countries, however, are far from reaching these goals.

Supplementary Materials Should Complement Textbooks

Using textbooks for instruction and using nontextbook instructional methods should be seen as complementary, not opposing approaches. Relevant reading materials about places and people with whom children can identify help make students interested and enthusiastic about reading. Broad reading advances students' vocabulary and comprehension skills. Supplementary readings also offer an educational experience that is connected with the world of the child. Well-selected books expose children to a variety of genre and situations likely to be found in real life.

But if a country can afford to finance only a limited number of books, textbooks—with all their drawbacks—may still be the most viable solution. Some criticisms of textbooks can be overcome and textbooks can be improved by introducing some of the more positive aspects associated with literature-based instructional reading approaches. Most important, textbooks can include more relevant, meaningful materials. They should, for instance, help children cope with such practical tasks as reading signs, commercial advertisements, labels, recipes, transportation schedules, bureaucratic forms, road maps, and instructional manuals of various kinds. Particularly in developing countries, teaching skills such as reading labels on medicine bottles in order to comfort sick children should take priority over using literature in the classroom. However, these are skills that are difficult to teach and that few students can master, even after five or six years of schooling (Eisemon, Patel, & Sena, 1987). This is because these practical uses of literacy are virtually ignored or given low priority in current primers, language textbooks, and the literacy books selected for use in schools. Young readers can be introduced to a variety of genres and literacy skills through carefully selecting samples to be included in textbooks. Literacy acquisition can be made more relevant by helping both teachers and students acquire skills in a less mechanical and more context-oriented environment fostered by creative textbooks.

In one of the first reviews of textbook issues in the developing world, Altbach (1983) noted that "nothing has ever replaced the printed word as the key element in the educational process, and, as a result, textbooks are central to schooling at all levels" (p. 315). In most cases, the only feasible option is to rely heavily on textbooks. Such books, however, should combine selected readings and appropriate activities typical of good instructional materials. The challenge is to use insights gleaned from experience and research to make better, more effective, relevant, and interesting textbooks.

References

Altbach, P.G. (1983). Key issues of textbook provision in the Third World. *Prospects*, 13, 315–325.

Anderson, L. (1984). The environment of instruction: The function of seatwork in a commercially developed curriculum. In G.G. Duffy, L.R. Roehler, & J. Mason (Eds.), *Comprehension instruction: Perspective and suggestions* (pp. 93–103). White Plains, NY: Longman.

Anderson, T.G., Armbruster, B.B., & Kantor, R.N. (1980). *How clearly written are children's textbooks—or bladderworts and alfalfa* (Reading Education Report No. 16). Champaign, IL: Center for the Study of Reading.

Askerud, P. (1993). *Strengthening the provision of basic learning materials in developing countries: Problems and issues.* Paper prepared for the Technical Consultation on Basic Learning Materials for Developing Countries. Paris: United Nations Educational, Scientific and Cultural Organization.

Bates, S. (1993). Battleground: One mother's crusade—the religious right and the struggle for control of our classroom. New York: Poseidon Press.

Clay, M. (1993). Language policy and literacy learning. In L. Limage (Ed.), *Language policy, literacy, and culture* (pp. 31–40). Paris: United Nations Educational, Scientific and Cultural Organization.

Coleman, J.S., Campbell, E.Q., Hobson, C.J., McPartland, J., Mood, A.M., Weinfeld, F.D., & York, R.L. (1966). *Equality of education opportunity*. Washington, DC: U.S. Government Printing Office.

DelFattore, J. (1992). *What Johnny shouldn't read: Textbook censorship in America*. New Haven, CT: Yale University Press.

Durkin, D. (1993). *Teaching them to read* (6th ed.). Boston, MA: Allyn & Bacon.

Eisemon, T.O., Patel, V., & Sena, O.S. (1987). Uses of formal and informal knowledge in the comprehension of instructions for oral rehydration therapy in Kenya. *Social Science and Medicine*, 25, 1225–1334.

Farrell, J.P., & Heyneman, S.P. (Eds.). (1989). *Textbooks in the developing world: Economic and educational choices*. Washington, DC: World Bank.

Harbison, R.W., & Hanushek, E.A. (1992). *Educational performance of the poor: Lessons from rural northeast Brazil*. New York: Oxford University Press.

Heyneman, S., & Loxley, W. (1983). The effect of primary school quality on academic achievement across twenty-nine high and low-income countries. *The American Journal of Sociology*, 88, 1162–1194.

Hauzer, R.F., Avella, M.V., Aponte, C., & Jaramillo, B. (1993). *Situació de los materiales educativos en la subregión andina*. Santafé de Bogotá: Secretariat for the Andres-Bello Agreement of Andean Pact Countries.

Oliveira, J.B. (1994). *How governments can distort markets—understanding textbook quality in the U.S.A.* (Economic Development Institute Working Papers, No. 94-37).Washington, DC: World Bank.

State of Florida. (1993). *Instructional Materials Committee on Training Materials*. Tallahassee, FL: State of Florida Department of Education.

Searle, B. (1985). *General operational review of textbooks*. Washington, DC: World Bank.

Tyson-Berstein, H. (1988). America's textbook fiasco: A conspiracy of good intentions. *American Educator*, 12(2), 20–39.

United Nations Educational, Scientific and Cultural Organization. (1991). *School fees and school books in state schools*. Paris: Author.

World Bank. (1991). *Africa book sector studies: Summary report*. Washington, DC: Author.

World Bank. (1993). *Asia region book investment review 1984–1995. Final Report*. Washington, DC: World Bank.

5 | Developing Local Publishing Capacity for Children's Literature

Tony Read

THE PROBLEMS ASSOCIATED with the development of adequate local publishing capacity in developing countries for children's literature are extremely complex. As Oliveira mentions in the previous chapter, in some countries it could take up to 15 years to build an infrastructure for textbook publishing and even longer for local trade book publishing. In this chapter I will address a number of the more basic problems and constraints that local publishers face.

Three basic factors determine the development of a local children's book publishing capacity:

1. the existence of viable markets that will attract and sustain publishing investment;

2. the availability of basic resources including working capital, authorship, illustrations, adequate prepress facilities, access to raw materials, and relevant manufacturing capacity to exploit and satisfy that market; and

3. the knowledge of professional skills (including market research, editorial, design, production, management, and financial skills) necessary to use resources profitably in the pursuit of the available market.

Existence of Viable Markets

Local publishing capacity cannot develop and sustain itself unless there is a market available to purchase books and magazines or at least to support their production. This is just as true of state publishing as it is of local commercial publishing. In Pakistan, for example, the parental market for children's books in local languages is very small (despite Pakistan's large population) and attracts little interest from either commercial or state publishers. Until recently, neither federal nor provincial authorities provided sufficient budgets to purchase supplementary reading materials for free distribution. There were no library or supplementary materials budgets to allow schools or districts to purchase materials from bookshops. The only Provincial Textbook Board (state-owned monopoly textbook publishers) that published supplementary materials did so because a bilateral aid agency provided funds to support publication. (Initially this project fully subsidized free distribution; eventually it hopes to subsidize publication for commercial sale.) It is not surprising that there have been few children's books published in local languages that are available in the market or the schools.

Parental Markets

Every country has two basic markets for children's books: the parental, or trade, market and the school and library market. In most developing countries the parental market is characterized by a large proportion of low-income families that place a low priority on non-textbook reading material; their expenditure budgets cannot accommodate such a purchase. A survey of primary school systems in 12 Asian countries (Read, 1992) concluded that 11 out of 12 countries had serious affordability problems in making even basic textbooks widely available. All 12 were seriously deficient in supplementary reading material provision in schools. If the educational system places little emphasis on the provision of textbooks and supplementary reading materials, it is not surprising that private purchase of supplementary reading materials has a low priority in parental budgets.

Where a parental market exists, it is often served by multinational children's book publishers in international languages rather than by local publishers in local languages. Again to cite Pakistani experience, this situation occurs in the flourishing private school market there, which operates largely in the English language. Significant chains of private schools have emerged, each of which makes substantial investments in school libraries and resource centers. Because private schools serve the educated and financial elite of the country, there is a demand for high-quality children's books imported from Western countries. Local children's book publishers are generally oriented to a less affluent market. They do not have the benefits of longer print runs and higher quality production of overseas multinationals and take on considerable financial risks by trying to compete. As a result, relatively little children's literature is published locally.

Other factors conspire to restrict the potential for publishing children's literature even where a trade market exists. For example, in some countries the number of retail bookshops has declined. Twenty years ago Sierra Leone had two retail bookshop chains, each with a dozen branches in provincial centers. After 15 years of economic difficulties,

In many developing countries, there is little children's literature published locally, so students often must read outdated or poorly written textbooks. © Paud Murphy. Used by permission.

Sierra Leone now has only one effective bookshop in the capital, Freetown. The remnants of the provincial chains have been gradually converted to basic stationery outlets and foodstuff stores. As a result of the bookshops' history of payment difficulties, publishers will now only accept cash for books; but storekeepers do not consider making a cash investment in children's books a sufficiently safe risk for their purposes. Outside Freetown children's books are no longer available, and retail outlets and publishers no longer have bookshops to market their books.

At least part of the reason for the decline in retail booksellers in many parts of the world is persistent donor investment in state publishing and distribution. Local publishers have become fewer in most developing countries in the past 20 years because the state (sometimes funded by donor agencies) has taken over the profitable publishing markets (such as primary school textbooks), which generate profits to invest in other types of publishing. Retail book selling has declined as the state has taken over direct distribution of textbooks into school systems and left the bookshops without sales. Without textbook sales to attract customers into the shops and to provide base turnover, there is neither profit nor other forms of incentive to stock and sell children's literature. This policy is in the process of changing, and an increasing number of donor projects now support competitive commercial publishing rather than state publishing, printing, and distribution.

Perhaps the most common phrase used in developing countries to explain low publishing output and low sales of children's books to parental or trade markets is that the country concerned has "no reading culture." It is argued that some cultural traditions are oral rather than literary and have been superseded by technologies such as the cinema, video, and radio. If this assertion is accepted, there is an implication that a reading society can be achieved only by attacking antireading cultural practices. However, it is at least as likely that reading is an undervalued activity in some countries simply because reading for pleasure has never been a part of the educational system.

Like the other authors in this book, I have repeatedly visited rural areas throughout the developing world and seen how little print material is actually available to children for pleasure reading in the schools. Most children have, at best, a part share in a textbook in poor condition; the book is frequently badly written, designed, and illustrated and has inadequate physical production specifications. Most schools in developing countries do not have supplementary reading material, as mentioned earlier. In some instances schools have books, but they are not available to children; I have seen many examples of reading books left in cupboards simply because the teachers have not been trained to use such material. Where community libraries exist, they are not always used. A community library in Nepal, which I visited in 1991, was not used by any school more than half a kilometer from the library. Most schools beyond that radius did not appear to know the community library existed.

Another reason some countries are considered to have no reading culture may be that prior to enrolling in school, few children in these developing countries are familiar with books. Few are aware that books have to be held in a certain manner to be read, that words have to be deciphered in a particular sequence, and that print and illustrations can be sources of knowledge and enjoyment. In developed countries, parental support for reading is recognized as a major contributor to the development of reading skills and important positive attitudes (Greaney, 1986), as mentioned in other chapters in this volume. Such support is exceedingly rare in developing countries—not an unexpected finding considering the lack of resources and the high level of parental illiteracy.

Under such circumstances, where print material for *any* purpose is not readily available and school and parental support for reading is rare, it is not surprising that nonreading cultures develop. Reading tends to be taught as a purely functional activity performed in the classroom or in a limited number of formal situations. Children can hardly accept reading as a stimulating leisure activity or as a source of self-improvement if they are not exposed to supplementary materials or if the system gives low priority to reading for enjoyment or to the development of a favorable attitude toward reading.

The problem is not necessarily financial. A recent survey of book availability among schools and parents (Read, 1994) in the Northwest Frontier Province of Pakistan indicated that 76% of parents would be prepared to contribute 10 rupees (approximately US$.30) each per year to buy books for a primary school book collection, if such a collection existed in schools. A total of 10 rupees, the equivalent of one-fifth of the daily rate of a contract day laborer, would be sufficient to purchase one reading book and would not represent an insupportable burden even for the poorest parents.

School and Library Markets

There has been a widespread decline in school library book and supplementary reading material provision in most developing countries over the past 30 years. In the 1950s and 1960s many developing countries made substantial investments in educational buildings, staff training, library stock, and management and supervision systems, which laid the basis for adequate levels of reading provision (Read, 1989). However, between the mid-1970s and the early 1980s a large proportion of these fledgling educational systems began to deteriorate. Investment in public library development, which also occurred in developing countries in the 1950s and 1960s, experienced a similar decline both in the local publishing of children's books and the provision of books in school classrooms.

The experience of one African country provides an example of the problems confronting school libraries. In the mid-1970s Sierra Leone had a thriving national library with a large children's section, 14 provincial and district libraries, and a mobile library service that visited schools regularly. Between 1975 and 1985 the effective book stock of the national library service in Freetown declined by almost 90%. Stock acquisition budgets shrank to almost nothing, library maintenance and extension budgets disappeared, the mobile library service collapsed, support services to schools ceased, and the library no longer represented a viable market for either local or overseas publishers. Funding had virtually disappeared. In 1972 the Sierra Leone government allocated 2 Leones per secondary school student for library stock acquisition. This represented, at that time, approximately US$5 per student at the prevailing exchange rates. By 1985 the exchange rate was 6 Leones to US$1 and by 1992 it was 500 Leones to US$1, but the library allocation was still 2 Leones per student. By 1992 the per-student allocation represented a fraction of a cent. Even this tiny sum was often not paid to the schools by the government (Bailor et al., 1987). This decline in library budgets and library provision occurred in many other countries that had adequate library and supplementary reading provision at the end of the 1960s but saw these systems in collapse by the end of the 1980s.

There are many reasons for the decline, but poor economic performance, rapidly rising inflation, constant currency devaluation, and shortages of foreign exchange for basic raw materials and essential imports, combined with expanding educational systems particularly at primary level, resulted in static or declining educational budgets. At the same time, the salary portion of the educational budgets in some developing countries became so dominant that there was little or no operational budget to allocate to basic supplies such as textbooks, school stationery, or library or supplementary reading materials. Figures from Sierra Leone suggest that salaries represented 72% of the total primary and secondary recurrent educational budget in 1975. By 1985, they had climbed to 98% of that budget.

Many countries that did not invest in libraries and supplementary materials during these initial years have never been in a position to afford them. Under these circumstances, it is evident that local publishing industries found it difficult to survive with the purchasing inability of one of its major markets—the library services.

Specific Conditions in Schools

A number of detailed school surveys undertaken recently offer detailed quantitative data on conditions relating to books and information in schools. Among the countries surveyed have been Albania, Brazil, Cambodia, Lesotho, Nepal, and Pakistan. The following excerpts from several of these studies illustrate the inadequacy of supplementary or library book provision.

Brazil

Supplementary reading materials are scarce everywhere except in a relatively few state schools where new library programs funded by donors are creating good libraries and reading rooms. The FAE (Foundation for Assistance to Students) supplementary reading materials program is only available to a limited number of municipal schools, but the supply of books is small and very irregular and there is very little or no teacher support or backup. The result is that stock is underused and deteriorates quickly. In most schools there are no supplementary readers of any kind. (Buchan, Bullock, & Read, 1993)

Cambodia

Fifty-five percent of schools visited had a library; 59% of these schools reported that the library was not used. On investigation the libraries consisted almost entirely of multiple copies of old textbooks for loan to students. Where nontextbooks occurred in school libraries they were overwhelmingly very old and irrelevant, and only one-third had books which could actually be read by the students since two-thirds of the books were in foreign languages (mainly French, English, and Russian) which the great majority of children could not understand. (Buchan et al., 1992)

Lesotho

Most primary schools visited had no supplementary readers in the sense that these would be expected to provide reading material which would extend and complement the reading contained in the course books. When asked about supplementary readers, many teachers and class teachers weren't sure of the meaning of the term, and the majority of those questioned assumed supplementary readers would consist of extra copies of pupils' textbooks.... The survey reported only 1% of primary schools with a school library or reading corner used by teachers and pupils. This 1% was entirely in the capital city. The survey also revealed that only 1% of primary schools have a community library within reasonable walking distance of the schools. The conclusion is that there is virtually no supplementary reading material available to any children in primary schools in Lesotho apart from a tiny minority of privileged urban children. (Keartland, 1992)

Nepal

No school had an atlas. Three schools had a simple Nepali dictionary, but in one of these the head teacher admitted that he had borrowed it recently from the DEO (District Education Officer) and would have to return it soon. One school had a simple English dictionary, which had also been borrowed from another school and would also have to be returned shortly. No school had a reasonable supply of supplementary readers. One school had some supplementary readers hung on a line across the head teacher's office. They were so dusty that they were obviously used very infrequently. The total number of supplementary readers in this school was 7 for a school of 200 children. No other school visited had evidence of any supplementary reader provision. (Buchan & Diwarkar, 1990)

School-Related Constraints on the Market

Studies in Africa, Asia, and Latin America have identified the following constraints.

Teacher resistance. A high proportion of both trained and untrained teachers have no experience using supplementary reading materials and trade books in the classroom. These teachers are entirely dependent on traditional textbook approaches and find free reading threatening because it could reveal their lack of subject knowledge. A change in attitudes is required.

Support. When supplementary reading materials or school libraries are introduced into systems where teachers have little previous experience, training and regular visits from supervisors are needed to provide support. This is particularly difficult to achieve in many countries in rural or inaccessible areas.

Administration. Poor management and a failure to organize the use, distribution, and loan of books are common features in school districts.

Cost. Maintaining even a minimal stock of supplementary reading materials at the primary level or in a basic school library at the secondary level is at least as expensive as basic textbook provision. As Oliveira mentioned in Chapter 4, in school systems that cannot afford basic textbooks, supplementary reading materials or libraries are considered to be a luxury.

Storage. There is a widespread lack of adequate storage facilities, particularly in primary schools. In many rural areas, shelving or weatherproof space for books is primitive or nonexistent. This inevitably leads to high rates of loss and damage to books and other materials and thus high-cost operations. There appears to be a need for book boxes, although the effectiveness of book boxes on the maintenance of book stock has not been adequately evaluated. A variety of book formats also causes severe storage problems in many schools. Consideration might be given to publishing a limited number of durable formats, which may be less attractive from a designer's or reader's point of view, but which nevertheless may be more practical for storage, durability, and cost purposes.

Distribution. A majority of school systems in developing countries have significant problems achieving adequate textbook distribution. For example, in 1991 the World Bank–funded Philippines Textbook Project failed to distribute 46% of the textbooks produced. Distributing large quantities of a limited number of textbook titles is much easier than distributing supplementary reading materials because smaller quantities of a much larger number of titles are usually involved.

Materials. Culturally relevant materials can be difficult to develop. This is particularly true when the books are required in minority languages in which there is little previous experience of authorship or publishing of children's books. Because library books normally will be supplied at the rate of one or two copies per school rather than a copy per student, publishers' print runs tend to be much lower and unit costs much higher, particularly when high-quality presentation and design are required to stimulate students' reading interest. In addition, when the main motivation for providing supplementary materials is curriculum support, the choice of titles and topics can be esoteric and often unappealing to children.

International Markets

Local publishers are confronted with stark choices concerning the nature of the markets that they should pursue. Frequently the choices seem mutually exclusive. The generally low per-capita incomes and small market size for children's books in many developing countries force local publishers into low-cost production. As a result, they are almost automatically cut off from the lucrative world coedition market (explained in the following paragraphs), the basis for most children's book publishing throughout the developed world. However, if local publishers pursued the high-quality coedition markets, they would almost certainly price their books out of their domestic market base.

Children's book publishers in the developed world benefit from their ability to extend print runs by selling into world language markets and by producing coeditions. (Producing coeditions extends print runs by overprinting a number of different language editions on identical color pages using the same print run.) Thus, a children's book publisher in the United Kingdom would expect to sell the original English-language version of a book in the United Kingdom, Ireland, Australia, New Zealand, and South Africa, plus smaller quantities to English-language markets throughout the world. The UK publisher probably would try to arrange a special American edition printed at the same time as the English edition and would attempt to add to the print run for French, German, Italian, Spanish, Japanese, and other language editions. To achieve this, a substantial investment needs to be made in preproduction artwork, design, and layout and in highly developed systems of marketing through maintaining close contacts with publishers who have similar interests. This investment results in a number of different publishers and countries sharing the benefit of common artwork, prepress work, and printing. Once the whole operation is established, a substantial proportion of the print run is presold, thus improving cashflow.

The situation in children's book publishing is radically different in the developing world. A children's book published in Nigeria, rooted in a Nigerian cultural context, often will not sell well in Ghana, or Kenya, or Zimbabwe. Sales of African-based cultural material to India and vice versa is equally difficult. The dominance of Western culture means that it is easier to sell *internationally* books that are based on a broadly defined and accepted Western culture or a neutral, internationally accepted culture than books that are based in any regional or national culture. Even where genuine regional language or cultural markets exist (for example, Swahili in East Africa or Bahasa in Indonesia and Malaysia), there are consistent barriers against cross-border sales, which can include tariffs or legal prohibition.

Although some Western countries have a strong interest in purchasing multicultural children's books, many local publishers in the developing world are not connected with the developed world coeditions network and have financial constraints (particularly foreign exchange availability) that prevent reliable cooperation in coedition printings. Further, these local publishers often produce book artwork, design, and film of inferior quality by Western market standards. There are honorable exceptions but in general the possibilities of print-run extension, which have been developed over the years by Western publishers to reduce unit costs, extend sales, and improve cashflow, are simply not yet available to the publishers of the developing world. This does not mean that print-run extension for developing countries could not be developed either as an adjunct to the existing international networks or as a parallel system operating with different and perhaps more appropriate standards.

Local publishing capacity in children's literature depends absolutely on the existence of not only a viable market but also a *stable* market. Markets can be small, but if they are reliable and continuous they can, under certain circumstances, be sustained. At first glance, donor investment, explained in Chapter 9 in this book, may appear to offer a solution to the problem of the dearth of interesting supplementary reading materials in developing countries. Unfortunately, this form of investment has tended to create an instantaneous, opportunistic market that is not continuous. Many donor book projects are based firmly on policies of fast-cash disbursement using complex procurement systems and documentation that are often unfamiliar to local publishers in developing markets. By the time local publishers have learned the bidding systems and have prepared to bid for publishing projects, the opportunity has often passed. The inability of donor agencies and governments to sustain investment in the book publishing sector over significant time periods contributes to the disinclination to invest in what is often seen as an ephemeral market opportunity for local publishers.

Donor tendering and procurement procedures for books are often complex and demanding and are more suitable for large multinational publishers who can specialize in developing bidding techniques through involvement in projects in many countries. Small local publishers with few resources and limited staff are often disinclined to bid even when they are encouraged to do so. External donor agencies need to spend more time training local publishers in bid submission procedures and in involving local book trades from the inception of projects so that they are informed at every stage of project development. Unfortunately local publishers are often the last to find out about donor-assisted projects.

The barriers to international selling and the difficulty of participating in the world coedition market inhibit local publishers in developing countries from fully exploiting the children's book market. Children's literature markets cannot be developed if parents and children never have access to suitable children's books. Publishing should be supported and developed as a starting point for market creation. However, the hostile market conditions existing in some developing countries discourage all but brave and foolhardy publishers from making significant investments that might not yield financial returns for several decades.

Availability of Resources

There are a number of key resource constraints in developing children's publishing capacity, which are described in the following.

Working Capital

A characteristic of local publishing in a majority of developing countries is a lack of investment finance. This is partly a result of depressed markets and low-level profit expectations. It is also caused by high interest rates on bank lending, banking systems that are less interested in small and middle-sized businesses, the lack of local risk capital and a widespread refusal to accept either publishers' stocks or work in progress as collateral for loans.

Publishing is essentially a human resource business with little investment in plant or equipment. The dominant investment is usually in stock or work in progress. The shortage of working capital means that advance payment for authors, investment in high-quality artwork, and expensive prepress processes are extremely difficult to afford. This forces publishers to concentrate on faster, lower cost and quality prepress processes and short cash cycles. Print runs tend to be cautious and therefore low, as mentioned earlier, and unit costs are often high as a result. This leads publishers to search for lower quality raw materials and manufacturing. Discounts and credit terms to distributors are also affected because expensive short-term money puts a premium on fast cashflow. As a result, existing trade retail outlets are often under stocked, and the demands of customers are not met. Publishers' development of sample material for evaluation by governments or aid agencies or for consideration for use in coedition sales also is difficult to finance for the same reasons.

Authorship and Illustrations

Most developing countries report difficulties in finding good authors and illustrators for textbooks and children's books. The majority of graphic design graduates from art schools and technical colleges in developing countries are oriented toward commercial work, advertising, or fine arts. Specific training in book illustration and design (including suitable typography) is rare.

Prepress Facilities

Many local publishers lack access to, or knowledge of, good quality prepress facilities. They are often isolated from international or regional information, so they are dependent on local facilities that may be substandard: ranges of formats and typefaces tend to be limited; film making and color separation processes are often of low quality; and inferior raw materials are commonly used.

Printing and Binding Facilities

Local production facilities also can be limited and substandard. Low-quality paper and cover material, poor finishing facilities, and inappropriate and low-quality binding are all problem areas. The consequences of poor-quality production are exacerbated by the difficult climatic and distribution conditions in many developing countries and

Developing local publishing capacity for children's literature is difficult in some areas because production facilities are limited. © Scott Walter. Used by permission.

are reflected in low durability and book life expectations of supplementary reading materials. Both durability and book life are key factors in the achievement of cost amortization, and thus industry sustainability.

Market Research

In developing countries there is often a consistent lack of appreciation of the nature of the market for books and supplementary reading material and its requirements, particularly in terms of language and interest levels and relevance to specific curricular requirements. Where publishing exists, there is a general tendency for a concentration on fiction and a lack of quality, nonfiction reference materials. Selection of titles is often undertaken by those who have no professional training in reading development or in children's literature. Frequently selection is more concerned with national, pedogogic, or religious values than with the identification of materials of inherent interest to children.

Knowledge of Skills

Professional skills training also is recognized as an urgent requirement for publishers in the developing world. Publishing industry skills training is heavily concentrated in developed countries such as Japan, the United States, and Western Europe. These include both short, inservice professional courses run by private organizations and one- to three-year diploma and degree courses run by institutions or universities. There are also some training courses based in developing countries. Although longer courses upgrade the level of entrants into the publishing industry, they are of little help to the working professional publisher who cannot afford to have key staff absent for long periods. The need for short-term, on-the-job training provided locally, or at least regionally, is preeminent. Professional attachment programs in which local publishers are provided with opportunities to work with experienced publishing houses also are relevant to the needs of publishers in developing countries.

The government publishing sector has been particularly resistant to upgrading by skills training. Civil-service posting systems and underpaid, demoralized staff are often a major barrier to the development of much needed publishing skills.

Training is required in the highly specialized sector of coedition publishing. Training in procurement and bid submission is a necessity for those who are interested in becoming involved in major donor agency projects. This is demonstrated by experience in the Sindh, Pakistan, Primary Education Development Project. A competition was announced for the procurement from local Pakistani publishers of 50 reading books by the Sindh Department of Education. The bid required the submission of either finished copies of existing books, or dummies and synopses of books in planning, or marked-up copies of overseas books for which translation and adaptation was intended. Despite a total budget allocation of almost US$1 million, only three publishers submitted bids covering 17 titles. The project planning documents specified that publishers were to be briefed before the announcement of the submission so that they could be trained in what was required and how they should prepare. Because of bureaucracy in the department, the publisher briefings were reduced to an informal two-hour meeting held months after its programmed date. As a result the majority of publishers declined to bid because they did not understand the tendering procedure and were unprepared, or unwilling, to submit books for selection in the form required.

The Future of Local Publishing in Developing Countries

In recent years there has been a rapid increase in government interest and donor investment in school library and supplementary materials projects. Countries that have on-going projects or projects in planning include Algeria, Bhutan, Brazil, Cambodia, Ghana, India, Indonesia, Jamaica, Jordan, Malaysia, Mozambique, Nepal, Nigeria, Pakistan, Papua New Guinea, Sierra Leone, South Africa, Tanzania, Uganda, and Zambia.

Some projects support publication in major world languages, whereas others focus specifically on regional or local languages. Some are concerned with fully subsidizing the production of supplementary reading material by state publishers for free distribution to schools; others support the purchase of existing materials for school libraries.

Some projects permit both foreign and local publishers to submit titles for selection; others are confined to local publishers. The majority of projects attempt to create a market and encourage local publishers to produce titles specifically for that market. With the notable exception of projects in Pakistan and Brazil, few projects include formal evaluations in their designs.

As mentioned, in most cases local publishers are provided with insufficient warning and instruction on how to prepare for developing and submitting material for selection in donor projects. In many cases they could benefit from conscious joint-venture arrangements with foreign publishers who have the skills and knowledge to assist but lack knowledge of local culture, language, and contacts. Even in joint ventures there is a need to help local publishers by providing independent contract and legal advice on the nature of cooperation and association with overseas companies.

Although many governments claim they want to create long-term sustainability in local publishing, often there are no commitments that governments will be able to continue to support publishing when donor support ceases. As the authors of this volume would agree, donor agency investment should be oriented more consciously toward market creation and long-term support for supplementary material and school library development, which in turn must lead to sustainability through government funding, perhaps in association with parental contributions.

If a market is created by aid agency investment and increasing government commitment, there is still a need to provide assistance to local publishing companies in the form of low-cost working capital, appropriate training, access to information on prepress and manufacturing sources and standards, contract and joint-venture advice, and author and illustrator training. Because many governments are reluctant to use loan money for training and technical assistance, support for these types of activities may have to be sought from other funding sources—namely, bilateral agencies and nongovernmental organizations.

If education is considered a high national priority then it should be reflected in support for the development of reading skills and habits. The development of reading skills and habits requires access to relevant, pedagogically sound, and interesting reading materials. For governments and donor agencies, the challenge is to include the promotion of reading and the creation of book access systems (both textbooks and supplementary reading materials) in educational development projects. To meet this challenge the major problems of developing a local publishing capacity for children's literature must be addressed: market creation and publishers' support and training. Both point to a natural area of partnership between multilateral agencies and governments on the one hand and bilateral and nongovernmental agencies on the other. This does not necessarily imply that governments and multilateral agencies have the responsibility to fund the provision of supplementary reading materials. When the many adverse circumstances in developing countries are considered, financing from governments may be impossible. However, governments and donor agencies combined with parental support can do much to create an environment in which children and students of all ages not only *can* read but also *will* read.

References

Bailor, M., Cohen, P., Jones-Parry, R., Read, A. & Simpkins, P. (1987). *Sierra Leone book sector study*. Prepared for the British Council and the Sierra Leone Ministry of Education. London: The Publishers' Association.

Buchan, A., Bullock, A., & Read, A. (1993). *Book provision in the Northeast region of Brazil*. Prepared for the Government of Brazil and the World Bank. London: International Book Development.

Buchan, A., & Diwarkar, D. (1990). *A primary school survey of Nepal*. Prepared for the Government of Nepal. London: International Book Development.

Buchan, A., Donaldson, M., Eastman, P., Keartland, E., Mello e Souza, A., & Read, A. (1992). *Cambodia book sector study*. Prepared for the Government of Cambodia. Ottawa, Ontario: Canadian Organization for Development Through Education.

Greaney, V. (1986). Parental influences on reading. *The Reading Teacher, 39*, 813–816.

Keartland, E. (1992). *A textbook and reading book survey of primary schools in Lesotho*. Prepared for the Government of Lesotho. London: International Book Development.

Read, A. (1989). *Textbook availability in the third world*. London: International Comparative Librarianship Group.

Read, A. (1992). *Asian region book investment review*. Paper prepared for the World Bank. London: International Book Development.

Read, A. (1994). *A school and parental survey of textbooks and supplementary reading materials in Northwest Frontier Province*. Paper prepared for United States Agency for International Development and the World Bank. London: International Book Development.

6 Promoting Independent Reading: Venezuelan and Colombian Experience

Nelson Rodríguez-Trujillo

IN RECENT YEARS many efforts have been made in Latin America (Odremán, 1992a) to introduce independent reading programs to foster the reading habit among school children. While researching for this chapter, I was able to identify more than 35 different programs in 14 countries. Odremán (1992b) includes the following countries and programs (number of programs in parenthesis): Argentina (2), Brazil (3), Colombia (5), Costa Rica (1), Cuba (1), Dominican Republic (1), Ecuador (6), Mexico (7), Panama (1), Perú (1), Uruguay (2), and Venezuela (4). Although some programs are of limited scope and coverage, others, particularly those in Colombia, Brazil, and Venezuela, address not only operational activities in schools and public libraries but also theoretical concepts of reading, teacher training praxis and methodology, classroom and library activities, research on children's literature, publishing policies and financing, and reading evaluation.

This chapter will describe some selected programs conducted in Venezuela and Colombia. I will include objectives and strategies of each program, present available evidence of each program's impact on the development of reading achievement levels or reading habits, and discuss the outcome of efforts to extend programs to the formal school system.

Theoretical Basis for Independent Reading Programs

Despite the differences in background and social setting that surrounded their conception, most independent reading programs in
Latin America and other countries seem to share several common assumptions (Ferreiro & Gómez, 1982; Ferreiro & Teberosky, 1979; Lerner,
1986; Lerner, Palacios, & Muñoz, 1989). In general there is broad
agreement on the following:

- Language is not a set of independent skills that can be learned
  by drilling and exercising in an environment void of meaning;
  rather, language constitutes an ability that has to be learned in
  social settings surrounded by relevant materials and activities.

- Reading materials should be available when needed for the
  development of language abilities and to satisfy children's interests. Children tend to be naturally motivated to find information in order to respond to self-generated questions. Availability of appropriate reading materials results not only in
  greater learning of content and the development of information searching skills, but also in personal satisfaction and positive attitudes toward learning (Guthrie & Greaney, 1991). In
  turn, these positive attitudes determine frequency of use of
  materials later in life.

- Learning to read, like any meaningful learning activity, is a complex self-generated process that requires respect for the intrinsic individual processes and time and opportunities to read.
  Teachers should not emphasize only the transmission of information to students; they should strive to create positive learning conditions by organizing a literacy environment that fos-
  ters use of reading materials, self-expression, writing, and
  communication.

- An independent reading approach requires teacher sensitivity
  to generate opportunities to learn. Teachers have to be trained
  in this approach and learn that there is much more to reading in
  the classroom than correct pronunciation or sounding out of
  words. Teachers should be readers themselves and have positive attitudes toward learning and reading.

Education in Venezuela and Colombia

In many respects the school learning situations in Venezuela and Colombia are similar to those found in most Latin American countries. Detailed analyses of both school systems are beyond the scope of this chapter (see Arboleda, Chiappe, & Colbert, 1991; Colbert, Arboleda, & Mogollón, 1977; Comisión Presidencial del Proyecto Educativo Nacional, 1986; Odremán, 1992a, 1992b; Organización de Estados Iberoamericanos para la Educación, la Ciencia y la Cultura, 1987; Rodríguez, N., 1991; Rodríguez-Trujillo, 1989; United Nations Children's Fund, 1994). However, the following conclusions can be drawn.

Every year, a large number of school-aged children are unable to enter school in Venezuela and Colombia. This figure has been estimated at up to 30% in certain areas (Arboleda, Chiappe, & Colbert, 1991; Organización de Estados Iberoamericanos para la Educación, la Ciencia y la Cultura, 1987; Venezuela Ministerio do Educación, 1990) and has been attributed to the lack of schools or to cultural, socioeconomic, or geographical factors. Among those who manage to enter the formal educational system there is a high attrition rate, ranging from about 35% in the first three grades in primary school and up to 45% in the first six grades. High attrition has been particularly pronounced in rural and marginal urban areas.

Education in schools is based on the verbal transmission and memorization of information; however, there is little opportunity to exchange, discuss, or question that information outside the classroom in real-life situations (Rodríguez, N., 1991). Teachers, of which about 20% do not have a teaching degree (Organización de Estados Iberoamericanos para la Educación, la Ciencia y la Cultura, 1987; Venezuela Ministerio de Educación, 1985a, 1990), are the basic source of information, and their authority is rarely questioned or challenged in the classroom. There is little incentive for students to think, reflect, or apply criteria to understand their world or solve everyday problems (Comisión Presidencial del Proyecto Educativo Nacional, 1986; Morles, 1983).

Similarly, little attention is given to personality, emotional and moral development, or development of social and communication skills (Comisión Presidencial del Proyecto Educativo Nacional, 1986).

There are few occasions for independent speaking, reading, or writing. Much of the classroom activity is teacher centered and has little relevance to children's interests (Morles, 1983; Rodríguez, N., 1991).

Reading materials are scarce and, when available, are limited to textbooks, many of questionable quality. Textbooks are used as the main and often the only source of the official curriculum. Access to other types of materials is difficult, and what is available tends to be expensive, of poor quality, and not related to children's interests (Betancourt & Rodríguez-Trujillo, 1986).

The teaching of reading is done by traditional methods, usually with children learning letters or syllables first and progressively constructing words and sentences that are drilled without reference to their meaning (Ferreiro & Teberosky, 1979; Lerner & Muñoz, 1986; Lerner, Palacios, & Muñoz, 1989; Rodríguez, M., 1991).

The limited available evidence suggests that reading achievement levels in some Latin American countries are low. The results of the International Association for the Evaluation of Educational Achievement Study of Reading Literacy in 32 countries (Elley, 1992), discussed in Chapter 2, showed that Venezuela, despite having a homogeneous population and a common home and teaching language, was among the lowest scoring countries and well below the expected level for its state of economic development. Unfortunately, no other Latin American country participated in the international reading study, so there is no basis for comparison.

Independent Reading Programs

School Libraries in Urban Venezuela

In 1961, after two years of democratic government and considerable investment in the expansion of the school system, educators realized that more than additional classrooms was necessary to improve education; lack of textbooks was a primary concern. The Banco del Libro, a private civil association financed by the private sector and the Ministry of Education, was established. It was viewed initially as a bank where the previous school year's textbooks could be exchanged by the students for the following year's books. Despite the success of this program, it was soon realized that the provision of textbooks was not enough and that effective learning requires access to a wide variety of reading materials and changes in educational practice.

In 1962, the Banco del Libro decided to develop a school library program, initially in 9 schools in Caracas. Subsequently in 1965 in Ciudad Guayana, an industrial city in southeastern Venezuela, a pilot program involving 7 schools was started. It gradually expanded until 1971 when all 38 public primary schools in the city had a library service supported by a public library system that included regular libraries, bookmobiles, and a center for teacher training, consulting, and research. The system included more than 38,000 students and 1,000 teachers. The program continued uninterrupted until 1982, when it was transferred to the Ministry of Education (Hung, 1980).

Various reports on the Guayana experience (Banco del Libro, 1964; Betancourt, 1964; Horowitz, 1972, 1974; Hung, 1980; Izaguirre, Pulido, & Briceño, 1977; Léidenz, 1971; Rodríguez-Trujillo, 1980; Uribe, 1989) showed many positive effects. For instance, different school library models were designed and attempted. These included the central school library, the classroom library, a rotating library, traveling boxes of books that are moved from classroom to classroom, and bookmobiles. Each was evaluated in terms of its relative effectiveness, cost, and viability. The central library was considered the most effective.

Books and book publishing became a field of study as a result of the Guayana experience. Standards of quality were established for physical characteristics, structure, and content. The perceived low quality of textbooks and children's books in general resulted in the creation of Ekaré, a highly successful children's book publishing house directly related to the Banco del Libro (Uribe, 1989).

Textbooks, instead of being considered the basic source of learning, were viewed in a more supportive role. Teachers and students accepted that the books should be complemented with materials such as information and reference books, literature, periodicals, booklets and leaflets, and nonprint materials (such as audiovisual materials, maps, and puppets).

The Guayana experience also directly influenced several important changes in student activities. Training in information-searching skills was emphasized. Teachers were expected not to rely on the textbook but to encourage their students to make use of a variety of other materials. Also, independent reading, especially of children's litera-ture, became an important part of the curriculum. Borrowing materials from the library was expected and became a feature of the program.

In addition, reports from Ciudad Guayana showed that the teacher came to be regarded as the administrator of activities and ex-periences in the classroom, rather than the basic source of informa-tion. Inservice training had increased teachers' technical skills and knowledge and changed their conceptions and attitudes toward learn-ing in general and reading in particular.

The evaluation reports, some of them based on anecdotal infor-mation and experts' opinions, indicate that the presence of the li-braries in the Ciudad Guayana schools allowed for an increase in read-ership, lower attrition rates, and higher levels of efficiency in primary school (Hung, 1980). The program, which had been confined to the first six grades of school, was extended because of the demand of sec-ondary school students; public libraries were created and became fre-quented places for completing school assignments and for recreation.

The Guayana experience also became a model for the education-al system and influenced the 1979 Presidential Decree, which led to the provision of libraries to public schools and the creation of the Na-tional School Library System. In 1992 this library system included more than 3,000 libraries operating with varied levels of success, as is the case today (J. D'Aubeterre, personal communication, 1992).

On a less positive note, the Guayana experience proved difficult to transfer to the regular educational system. The program was too expensive to reproduce and expand, and its practices were difficult to incorporate into everyday classroom activity. It eventually became ev-ident that independent reading programs have to form an integral part of the educational system from the earliest grades in order to be suc-cessful, and that efforts to expand successful programs have to make provision for inservice teacher training.

The Rural School Library Experience in Venezuela

Out of more than 15,000 schools in Venezuela, approximately 7,000 are in rural areas, and 3,500 are one-teacher schools with 10 to 50 students (Venezuela Ministerio de Educación, 1985a, 1985b, 1990). In rural areas the problems of illiteracy are particularly pronounced;

the population lacks not only reading materials but also the means to obtain them. In 1982 the Banco del Libro, based on its library development experience in urban schools, started a program to establish book collections in a small number of one-teacher rural schools (Banco del Libro, 1986).

At the outset an action research model was developed. Substantial information on rural education, one-teacher schools, and in particular, school and classroom practices was gathered. As a second step, reading and some nonprint materials were placed in four schools in which classroom observations were conducted over two years. From this experience, a model school library was developed and a training course for teachers designed (D'Aubeterre & Melfo, 1986). Between 1984 and 1987, with funds provided by the Organization of American States and private sources, 126 libraries were installed and approximately 240 teachers, principals, and supervisors received training in library usage.

The rural library program sought to (1) create a literacy environment in both the school and the community; (2) improve the quality of the educational process by providing relevant materials when and where needed; (3) support rural extension, agricultural development programs, and literacy campaigns by providing materials from its basic collection; and (4) support the professional improvement of teachers by offering basic training in library usage, providing reading materials, and fostering communication among teachers in the program (Rodríguez-Trujillo, 1986).

The basic collection included the following:

- Printed materials: 20 textbooks; 40 nonfiction books; 70 fiction books; 10 reference books (dictionaries, an atlas, an almanac, the Venezuelan Constitution, and relevant laws); and 30 booklets dealing with agricultural production, health, law, community organization, conservation, and cooperative movement.
- Nonprint materials: maps, a globe, a radio cassette player, and one set of materials for literacy campaigns.
- Materials needed to set up the library, such as a bookshelf, a carrying case for book exhibitions and transport, bookends, and reading promotion posters.

Teacher training was performed in 32-hour workshops and focused on types of classroom materials and their efficient use in the teaching process, development of students' reading habits and research skills, determination of informational and recreational needs of the community and the provision of reading materials, and strategies for increasing the collection (Campos, 1984). During the workshop, teachers were required to read as many materials as possible from the library. Working in small groups, they also had to plan a one-day program for their schools, taking into account the need to attend to several grades simultaneously.

As part of the evaluation process, workshops were held with the teachers one year after the school began in the program (D'Aubeterre & Melfo, 1986). The following school and community effects were identified:

- School practices had changed and students had become more active in the learning process.
- Children borrowed freely, thus expanding the influence of the library to the community.
- The community became aware of the presence of the library and the importance of the school and the teacher.
- People discussed books and their characters in conversation. In one area during the school vacation, the community requested that the library be moved to the health center, where the teacher trained the nurse to maintain the lending activity. Thus, it can be assumed that books became valued by people who had not had contact with them before.

The evaluation also underlined the difficulties of introducing independent reading approaches into schools with rigidly defined traditions and practices. Acceptance of an independent reading approach required substantial teacher attitudinal change and an adoption of school practices based on a different conception of reading, which could not be achieved in the 32-hour workshop. Additional contacts and communication were considered necessary to guarantee a more permanent effect.

Some library-support strategies for rural areas were redefined after 1989. The library was no longer necessarily placed in the school, but wherever its effect could be maximized (S. Rojas, personal communication, 1992). The installation, maintenance, and development of the library became a community matter from the beginning, although teachers remained involved. Training of teachers and community members included several workshops organized over an extended period and dealt with themes such as "collective development of knowledge," "learning from experience," and "community diagnosis." Each library was assigned to a "pilot library," which served as a demonstration center, arranged meetings and workshops, collected writings on oral traditions, and in general supported the more isolated libraries. Since 1989, libraries have been installed in 63 communities in three Venezuelan states, with support from international and private enterprises such as United Nations Children's Fund, Caritas International, oil companies, and coffee growers' organizations. In the interim, training has been provided for 81 librarians, community members or members of social action institutions, 170 teachers, and 63 school principals (Rojas & García, 1993).

Venezuela's Plan Nacional Lector—National Reading Plan

The National Reading Plan (NRP) was conceived in 1989 and developed by the National Commission on Reading as an alternative to the traditional methodology of teaching reading and writing in the first three grades in basic education (Comisión Nacional de Lectura, 1992; Odremán, 1992a, 1993). Its design was influenced by the outcomes of the school library programs described in the previous sections, publishing experience in children's books (Uribe, 1989), and theoretical developments in reading (Ferreiro & Teberosky, 1979; Lerner & Muñoz, 1986; Lerner, Palacios, & Muñoz, 1989). It also sought to make use of the infrastructure of the National Public Library System.

NRP grew out of the general concern with the high attrition rate in the first three grades in primary school, the low level of reading ability of these early dropouts, and the failure of the prevailing teaching methods to develop reading skills and long-term interest in reading. The main objectives of NRP were to develop reading comprehension and writing skills, improve school learning, and reduce dropout rates related to poor reading skills (Odremán, 1992a). The underlying philosophy of the program accepted that reading can be learned only by actually reading, that learning must be associated with pleasure and access to a variety of interesting and attractive books in an environment of freedom of choice (Odremán, 1992a).

A basic library book collection consists of 27 children's literature books: nine books for each of grades one to three. Two different basic collections have been developed so far; more will be created in the future. Books are accompanied by manuals that explain their content and suggest individual and group activities. Each month during the school year, a participating teacher receives one box containing 40 books of the same title, so that all children in the classroom read the same book. Public libraries in each community have participated in the organization, storage, and distribution of boxes; in addition, 40 public librarians have been trained to orient teachers and help with the program.

Teachers are invited, either by newspaper notices or by other teachers in the NRP program, to attend reading workshops. Those who show interest during the workshop are selected for the program and participate in a five-day training session that includes the psychology of language, the process of reading and writing, and the foundations and structure of the school curriculum. Particular attention is devoted to the content of the books and manuals included in the NRP. Participating teachers meet every three months during the school year to share and discuss their experiences, get additional training, and read children's literature. The inservice teacher training component has become one of the strengths of the program; it has consolidated a communication process that supports participants.

Classroom activities promoted by the NRP are designed to create a literacy environment. During the first week of school students are expected to relate to the book in a free atmosphere. They can simply look at it, read it if they have the ability, and share their experiences. The teacher organizes storytelling sessions based on the book and encourages students to speak about the characters or change the end or the beginning of the story to see how the story is affected. During the second week, didactic elements are introduced with emphasis on reading and writing skills, reading aloud to one another, representing the characters in the story, or writing a different end to the story. During the third and fourth weeks, each student is expected to share the book with the family at home.

Three formative evaluation studies, based on questionnaires directed to students, parents, teachers, and librarians, were conducted (Odremán, 1993). Results suggested that the program resulted in greater integration of the school, the public library, and the community. Teachers considered that participating students were reading better than before and were able to write about a variety of themes. Students visited public libraries more, and they considered that they had improved their school performance, participated more in classroom activities, and had enriched their oral language. Parents indicated that they participated more in the reading and writing activities of their children by sharing the books they bring home. Teachers perceived that their concepts of learning and reading had improved and that they

Independent reading programs developed in rural areas have changed school practices and emphasized the importance of reading for pleasure. © Pamela Winsor. Used by permission.

had been encouraged by the program to read other books, make class-room activities more interesting, and pursue further activities. In 1995 the Universidad de los Andes began a summative evaluation study to determine the effects of the program on children's reading ability; this study is still in progress.

The pilot phase of the NRP involved more than 124,000 children and 5,000 teachers in all Venezuelan states, and it covered approximately 8% of the student population in grades one to three. Between 1994–1996 it was expanded to 250,000 students and more than 8,000 teachers. The extension plan foresees that all Venezuelan students in grades one to three will be included in the program by 1999. Also, financed by the World Bank and the Interamerican Development Bank, an experimental extension is being conducted to include all sections in grades one to three in selected schools in seven states, including more than 112 schools and more than 22,000 students. Two further pilot programs are being conducted to determine how NRP can be extended to include students in grades four to nine. The four-year pilot phase of the NRP was completed in 1994 and is being analyzed. Provided that the results are satisfactory, the program will be extended to the whole public primary school system.

To date the cost of the program has been paid for by the Venezuelan Congress, the Ministry of Education, and more recently by the World Bank and the Interamerican Development Bank. Fifty percent of the budget is spent on books and materials, 35% on training and travel expenses, and 15% on administration. These costs are relatively low because of the extent of voluntary participation and the use of the existing public library infrastructure (Odremán, 1993; L. Carrera, personal communication, 1996).

Colombia—Escuela Nueva

Colombia has experienced a number of different initiatives with independent reading programs. Among the more notable are the programs developed by Fundalectura, Colcultura, and the National Reading Plan, sponsored by the Colombian First Lady's office. The Escuela Nueva program is of particular significance.

In 1961 the Colombia Ministry of Education, concerned about the inadequacies of the educational system in rural areas, initiated a program to create one- and two-teacher rural schools in one province. The program expanded steadily until 1975, when Escuela Nueva was firmly established (Arboleda, Chiappe, & Colbert, 1991; Colbert, Arboleda, & Mogollón, 1977; Schiefelbein, 1992). Over time it has become a model for rural education both in Colombia and in other Latin American countries (Arboleda, Chiappe, & Colbert, 1991).

Observations and studies had led the Colombian authorities to conclude that the educational system as it operated might not be appropriate for rural students. First, large numbers of students work in the fields during planting and harvesting time, resulting in long periods of school absenteeism. Second, the traditional school curriculum, developed for urban settings, had little meaning for rural students, which contributed to low achievement levels and eventually led to students' permanently leaving school. Third, teachers who had urban backgrounds tended to be insensitive to rural lifestyles, and they had neither the experience nor the time to adapt or develop materials appropriate for rural areas.

Escuela Nueva was designed to address these problems. Its objectives are (1) to improve qualitatively and quantitatively basic education in rural areas and (2) to extend education from third to the fifth grade of basic education. Escuela Nueva's basic principles include the following:

- active, meaningful, student-centered learning;
- a flexible curriculum adjusted to the student's ability and to labor demands during the planting and harvesting seasons;
- close connection between school and community, with teachers learning from the community and community members establishing close ties to the school; and
- emphasis on four basic learning needs—language (both reading and writing), mathematics, citizenship, and learning from the child's immediate and cultural environmental circumstances.

As part of the basic training program, teachers participate in four one-week workshops designed to transmit the necessary skills to manage several grades simultaneously, improve relations with the community, and learn about the content and methodology applied in Escuela Nueva. Library usage is a common workshop topic. Three-month intervals are allowed between workshops to facilitate classroom experimentation and sharing of experience among fellow teachers. The workshop methodology is similar to one the teachers are intended to use with the students and is designed so that teachers experience problems and difficulties similar to those the children in classrooms confront. The teachers learn to adapt various methods and materials and to monitor and learn from changes. They are encouraged to trust their own intuitions and ideas and to learn from their experiences and from the immediate reality in the community. They are also expected to express their learning in writing, so that it can be shared with other teachers and community members.

The materials and facilities used in the Escuela Nueva program are listed here:

- manuals for teachers and for students;
- a methodological guide for teaching reading, writing, and math that emphasizes rural realism and practical applications;
- guides for students and teachers that substitute for textbooks (from second grade on, the materials are self-administered, thereby allowing children who withdraw from school, who work during planting or harvesting seasons, or who move with their family to other locations to continue where they left off when they return to school);
- a school library of 100 titles (reference, textbooks, children's literature, and documentary materials); and
- three "Learning Corners" for math, social sciences, language, and science.

Students are expected to participate actively in the learning process and be responsible for their own learning. Each student is furnished with guides made of low-cost materials, designed for independent learning and independent mastery of learning objectives. Students are expected to interact closely with other classmates, the teacher, and community members. Older or higher achieving students are expected to support newer or younger classmates. Learning is directed toward real-life situations and activities in the students' immediate environment. Students participate in school government and in committees responsible for maintenance and cleaning, newspaper and library, recreation, sports and the school garden.

Escuela Nueva students have had a much higher level of self-esteem than those in more traditional schools, which is attributed to the more participative practices in Escuela Nueva (Arboleda, Chiappe, & Colbert, 1991). They also have shown higher scores on measures of sociocivic behavior, self-esteem, and selected subjects such as mathematics for third grade and Spanish for third and fifth grades (Psacharopoulos, Rojas, & Velez, 1992).

The experience was sufficiently positive at the local and departmental levels to justify the extension of the Escuela Nueva approach to the rest of the Colombian rural school system. Since 1985 great efforts have been made to establish Escuela Nueva as the basic program for rural education, covering approximately 27,000 schools and 60,000 teachers. This expansion process has not been without difficulties, however. The evaluation study (Arboleda, Chiappe, & Colbert, 1991) noted that many decisions about the program were based primarily on quantitative and financial concerns rather than on technical criteria, thus reducing its effectiveness. The study also showed that the demand for training exceeded the capacity of the program to respond, supervision was not performed, and at times there was failure to provide learning materials on time. In addition, much of the success of Escuela Nueva depended on the level of support given by local administrators.

Evaluation Studies

The Venezuelan and Colombian programs included evaluation studies to determine their effectiveness and to identify corrective strategies. Most studies were based either on surveys, anecdotal information, or experts' opinions. The exceptions are two Venezuelan studies that explored the effects of access to reading materials on the reading behavior and ability of children (Rodríguez-Trujillo, 1984) and one evaluation study of Escuela Nueva (Psacharopoulos, Rojas, & Velez, 1992).

In one of the Venezuelan studies (Rodríguez-Trujillo, 1984), 24 sixth-grade classrooms (694 students) were randomly selected in 12 schools, located in three different cities. Six of the schools had a library and 6 did not. All served working-class students. The sampling procedure was designed to control for socioeconomic status as well as other services the schools offered, such as sports facilities. Measures of reading comprehension, vocabulary, information-searching skills, and content area kowledge were obtained through objective tests. A self-administered questionnaire was used to obtain information on reading behavior (such as how much the students liked reading and the amount and quality of books, newspapers, and magazines read). Responses on the questionnaire were used to compute a reading habit index (RHI). Results showed a significant positive relation ($p < 0.01$) between the RHI and availability of a school library, with a significantly higher proportion of the heavy readers attending schools with a library. Students in schools with libraries also showed significantly higher scores on vocabulary, information-searching skills, and reading comprehension tests; however, they did not score highly on curriculum information tests.

Students were asked to identify one person who had influence on their reading. Teachers who could be classified as "readers" (on the basis of the number of books and other materials they had read in the six previous months) in schools with libraries were mentioned significantly more often as influential people than those classified as "nonreaders" in similar schools and also more often than those classified as "readers" in schools without a library.

The second study (Rodríguez-Trujillo, 1984) was confined to sixth-grade students in a large school in which a library was about to be installed. Measures of reading comprehension and vocabulary were obtained at the beginning and end of the school year. Again a reading habit index was computed, and a separate reading ability index (RAI) was created by averaging the comprehension and the vocabulary transformed test scores. Results showed a tendency for all students to increase their readership in absolute terms—all of them read more by the end of the school year. In relative terms, those who increased their readership most showed highest scores on the RAI. The group classified as nonreaders both at the beginning and end of the school year recorded the lowest RAI scores. Students who recorded initial high RAI scores but low RHI scores improved their reading habits substantially once they were given access to reading material. Those with initial low RAI scores made less progress in developing the reading habit. For these students separate skills development treatment may be necessary before they can capitalize on the benefit of having access to supplementary reading material.

A 1987 an evaluation of Escuela Nueva was conducted by the Colombian Ministry of Education (Psacharopoulos, Rojas, & Velez, 1992) to determine the achievement levels of third and fifth graders in mathematics, Spanish, self-esteem, creativity, and civic behavior. A total of 168 Escuela Nueva and 60 traditional schools were included in the sample of more than 3,000 students. Cognitive achievement tests in Spanish and mathematics were administered, as were measures of self-esteem, creativity, and civics. Questionnaires were used to generate information on the characteristics of students, teachers, and schools. The mean scores for the cognitive tests revealed that Escuela Nueva students scored higher than traditional school students, except in mathematics at the fifth-grade level. On the noncognitive variables, the mean scores were also higher for Escuela Nueva students, who showed a lower tendency to declare they would withdraw from school the following year. Within the Escuela Nueva sample, comparisons showed that factors associated positively with academic performance were gender (males did better in math and females in Spanish), owning a television, and having books at home. Other variables such as experience, education, and place of residence of a student's teacher also correlated strongly with cognitive outcomes. The authors conclude from previous research (Rojas & Castillo, 1988) that Escuela Nueva achieved beneficial results at a cost per student that does not differ substantially from that of traditional schools.

Final Comments

Despite the lack of studies providing substantial data, it can be said that the independent reading programs described in this chapter have been successful overall. They have reached their objectives of improving reading ability or reading habits among students, providing inservice training to teachers, involving parents in their children's education, and generating interest within the educational system in reading as something more than decoding skills.

However, most of these independent reading programs were limited in their scope and population coverage. As long as conditions were controlled, and the number of teachers and students involved limited, difficulties were overcome and objectives generally attained. Problems arose when the programs were extended to a larger population, when it became necessary to reach less controlled groups, or when the program was introduced into traditional educational systems. Problems of such magnitude may give the impression that independent reading programs are difficult to implement with large populations. The Venezuelan experience with school libraries both in urban and rural settings provides good examples of this.

Lessons learned from the Guayana experience in Venezuela and Escuela Nueva in Colombia (Arboleda, Chiappe, & Colbert, 1991) suggest that preconditions for expanding a program to include the whole population include the following:

- sufficient funds to reach the larger population;
- political commitment to support the effort;
- demonstration models that work well in various regions simultaneously;
- appropriate administrative methods;
- a transitional process based on admitting errors, learning from them, and establishing a clear link between knowledge-building and action;
- a core team that works during the initial stages and moves to positions of leadership during the expansion period;
- teacher training viewed as an ongoing process; and
- supervisors that assume the role of trainers of teachers, thus legitimizing the innovations in the classroom and its environment.

In Latin America many children simply do not learn to read and write, or their comprehension level is so low that they are functionally illiterate (Ferreiro & Teberosky, 1979). But Latin American countries require populations that are able to read in order to sustain their development process and produce and maintain the high-technology products and systems that are needed today (such as automobiles, computers, communication equipment, televisions, and medical equipment). The significance of reading for the workplace was underscored in a study of automobile mechanics (Rodríguez-Trujillo & Feliú, 1987) that established that, contrary to popular wisdom, mechanics in the course of their work are required to perform information searches, consult reference materials, transform data from imperial to metric units and vice versa, and read complex dials, specifications, and technical manuals. However, few of the skills required by these activities are taught or practiced in schools, and many mechanics do not complete school.

Limiting reading materials to textbooks in schools is insufficient when the demands of modern society are considered; although, as Oliveira stressed in Chapter 4, providing nontextbook materials is often a difficult task for many developing countries. The provision of a wide variety of reading materials, and the freedom to select, read, comment, and interact among peers are recognized important components of independent reading programs. Classroom practices will have to be changed and teachers will have to be trained to accept a concept of reading that is different from the traditional notion that reading means mastering decoding skills. Future programs will have to emphasize that children must read for information, understanding, and pleasure.

References

Arboleda, J., Chiappe, C., & Colbert, V. (1991). The new school program: More and better primary education for children in rural areas in Colombia. In H. Levin & M. Lockheed (Eds.), *Effective schools in developing countries* (pp. 58–76). Washington, DC: World Bank.

Banco del Libro. (1964). *Banco del Libro develops an experimental school library system in Ciudad Guayana.* Caracas, Venezuela: Author.

Banco del Libro. (1986). *Proyecto de provisión de recursos para el aprendizaje e información las escuelas rurales unidocentes.* Caracas, Venezuela: Author.

Betancourt, V. (1964). *Plan general del Banco del Libro sobre difusión de bibliotecas escolares.* Caracas, Venezuela: Banco del Libro.

Betancourt, V., & Rodríguez-Trujillo, N. (1986). *Situación de la lectura y la escritura en Venezuela.* Paper presented to the Comisión Nacional para el Estudio de un Proyecto Educativo Nacional, Caracas, Venezuela.

Campos, M. (1984). *Propuesta de un programa de capacitación para el docente de escuelas rurales unitarias en el manejo y uso de los recursos para el aprendizaje.* Unpublished thesis. Caracas, Venezuela: Universidad Central de Venezuela, Escuela de Bibliotecología.

Colbert, V., Arboleda, V., & Mogollón, O. (1977). *Hacia la Escuela Nueva*. Bogotá, Colombia: Carvajal S.A.

Comisión Nacional de Lectura. (1992). *Proyecto plan lector de cajas viajeras*. Project presented to sponsors. Caracas, Venezuela: Author.

Comisión Presidencial del Proyecto Educativo Nacional. (1986). *Informe al Presidente de la República Dr. Jaime Lusinchi*. Caracas, Venezuela: Author.

D'Aubeterre, J., & Melfo, H. (1986). *El Banco del Libro y su acción en las areas rurales*. Guayana, Venezuela: Banco del Libro.

Elley, W. (1992). *How in the world do students read?* Hamburg, Germany: International Association for the Evaluation of Educational Achievement.

Ferreiro, E., & Teberosky, A. (1979). *Los sistemas de escritura en el desarrollo del niño*. Mexico City: Siglo XXI.

Ferreiro, E., & Gómez, P.M. (1982). *Nuevas perspectivas sobre los procesos de lectura y escritura*. Mexico City: Siglo XXI.

Guthrie, J.T., & Greaney, V. (1991). Literacy acts. In R. Barr, M.L. Kamil, P.M. Rosenthal, & P.D. Pearson (Eds.), *Handbook of reading research: Volume II*, (pp. 68–96). White Plains, NY: Longman.

Horowitz, R. (1972). *Consideraciones sobre la elaboración de normas para los servicios bibliotecarios escolares*. Caracas, Venezuela: Banco del Libro.

Horowitz, R. (1974). *La biblioteca escolar en Venezuela: Un modelo de servicios bibliotecarios escolares para un país en vías de desarrollo*. Caracas, Venezuela: Banco del Libro.

Hung, L. (1980). *El Programa de servicios bibliotecarios escolares de Ciudad Guayana*. Paper presented at the International Association of School Librarians Ninth Annual Conference, Ciudad Guayana, Venezuela.

Izaguirre, I., Pulido, M., & Briceño, R. (1977). *El desarrollo de servicios bibliotecarios en Venezuela: Estrategia y alternativas de transferencia de la experiencia de Guayana*. Caracas, Venezuela: Banco del Libro.

Léidenz, M. (1971). *La experiencia del Banco del Libro en servicios bibliotecarios escolares*. Caracas, Venezuela: Banco del Libro.

Lerner, D. (1986). La relatividad de la enseñanza y la relatividad de la comprensión: un enfoque psicogenético. *Lectura y vida*, Año 6, 2, 10–13.

Lerner, D., & Muñoz, M., (1986). *La lectura: Concepciones teóricas y perspectivas pedagógicas*. Caracas, Venezuela: Ministerio de Educación.

Lerner, D., Palacios, A., & Muñoz, M. (1989). *Comprensión de la lectura y expresión escrita de niños alfabetizados: Experiencia pedagógica*. Buenos Aires, Argentina: Aique Grupo Editor.

Morles, A. (1983). *Habilidades a desarrollar en una educación para el futuro*. Caracas, Venezuela: Cinterplan.

Odremán, N. (1992a). Programas de la Comisión Nacional de Lectura en Venezuela. *Lectura y vida*, Año 12, 2, 17–28.

Odremán, N. (1992b). *Elementos estratégicos para el diseño, formulación, ejecución y evaluación de políticas nacionales de lectura en América latina y el Caribe*. Caracas, Venezuela: Comisión Nacional de Lectura.

Odremán, N. (1993). *Plan lector de cajas viajeras: Un proyecto para promocionar la lectura en las escuelas Venezolanas*. Caracas, Venezuela: Comisión Nacional de Lectura.

Organización de Estados Iberoamericanos para la Educación, la Ciencia y la Cultura. (1987). *Sistema de indicadores socioeconómicos y educativos*. Madrid: Author.

Psacharopoulos, G., Rojas, C., & Velez, E. (1992). *Achievement evaluation of Colombia's Escuela Nueva: Is multigrade the answer?* Washington, DC: World Bank.

Rodríguez, M. (1991). *La promoción de la lectura en Venezuela*. Paper presented to the 3rd Congreso Latinoamericano de Lectoescritura, Buenos Aires, Argentina.

Rodríguez, N. (1991). *La educación básica en Venezuela* (2da edición). Caracas, Venezuela: Ediciones Dolvia.

Rodríguez-Trujillo, N. (1980). *Introducción a las ponencias*. Paper presented at the International Association of School Librarians Ninth Annual Conference, Ciudad Guayana, Venezuela.

Rodríguez-Trujillo, N. (1984). *Papel de la escuela y la familia en la formación de hábitos de lectura*. Caracas, Venezuela: Banco del Libro.

Rodríguez-Trujillo, N. (1986). *Provision of reading materials and learning resources to rural school*. Paper presented at the International Association of School Librarianship Fifteenth Annual Conference, Nova Scotia, Canada.

Rodríguez-Trujillo, N. (1989). *El Acceso a la información impresa, audiovisual y de almacenaje electrónico*. In *Recursos para el aprendizaje en la educación formal y no formal*. Caracas, Venezuela: Congreso Nacional de Educación.

Rodríguez-Trujillo, N., & Feliú, S.P. (1987). *Modelo de selección para mecánicos automotrices*. Caracas, Venezuela: Psico Consult.

Rojas, C., & Castillo, Z. (1988). *Evaluación del programa Escuela Nueva en Colombia*. Research report from Instituto SER de Investigación, IFT-133, Processed, Bogotá, Colombia.

Rojas, S., & García, G. (1993, November). *La experiencia del Banco del Libro en el medio rural*. Paper presented to the Encuentro de Investigadores en el Area de Lectura y Escritura, II Feria Internacional del Libro de Caracas.

Schiefelbein, S. (1992). *En busca de la escuela del Siglo XXI*. Paris: United Nations Educational, Scientific and Cultural Organization.

United Nations Children's Fund. (1994). *Estado mundial de la infancia*. Barcelona, España: J. y J. Asociados.

Uribe, V. (1989). *La producción del libro recreativo en Venezuela*. In *Recursos para el aprendizaje en la educación formal y no formal*. Caracas, Venezuela: Congreso Nacional de Educación.

Venezuela Ministerio de Educación. (1985a). *Memoria y cuenta 1984*. Caracas, Venezuela: Author.

Venezuela Ministerio de Educación. (1985b). *Informe de la Comisión Nacional para el Desarrollo de la educación rural*. Caracas, Venezuela: Author.

Venezuela Ministerio de Educación. (1990). *Memoria y cuenta 1990*. Caracas, Venezuela: Author.

7 | Promoting Children's Book Publishing in Anglophone Africa

Scott Walter

TO DEVELOP THE reading habit, children must learn to love reading. From an early age children need to encounter as wide a variety of books as possible—books that entertain, arouse interest, and excite their curiosity. In much of Africa, as in other developing areas of the world, where a few textbooks may be the only reading materials found in the classroom, children often miss the opportunity to read for enjoyment, which results in their reading skills being severely underdeveloped. Because these children cannot read well enough to understand printed matter, textbooks can become a source of discouragement rather than a source of knowledge. The consequences may be severe: students may develop an aversion to reading. Further, upon leaving the primary school system, they graduate into an almost bookless society. With little access to books and other reading materials, these graduates may lose their limited ability to read and write, resulting in continued high-level illiteracy and, therefore, at least a partial waste of the state's investment in public education.

Success in promoting reading depends on access to appropriate literature, which ultimately is made possible by the development and promotion of an active, indigenous book trade, as supplied by entrepreneurial, indigenous publishers. As Read argues in Chapter 5, developing local book publishing capacity depends primarily on the existence of a viable market, but if neither market nor capacity presently exists, state and donor purchasing power must be directed to bolstering demand for books. First, however, the product must be introduced, and for this product to be diversified, sustainable, and respectful of the cultural integrity of developing countries, it must originate from a diversity of local independent publishers. In addition, for the product to be accessible to children throughout the country, it must be distributed through a nationwide system of wholesalers and retailers.

In this chapter I will discuss how local publishing capacity is determined and present some guiding principles to be considered in publishing, which will facilitate a sustained book supply. I also will outline promising programs and initiatives in several African countries that support these principles and demonstrate how children can gain access to entertaining, exciting, and educational books. To conclude, several suggestions for how the children's book publishing industry in Africa can progress successfully are offered.

Determining Publishing Capacity

Africa's present "book famine" has been caused largely by the decision of governments and donors to ignore local independent publishers, to allow only state-run publishing, and to import large quantities of books from Europe. The existence of a single government textbook publisher deprives independent publishers and booksellers of their most lucrative markets. It results in the industry becoming bureaucratic and debilitated by subsidies while denying it the dynamic entrepreneurial skills it requires. Directing funds into large book importations from Europe has served in the long run only to guarantee a healthier European publishing industry because the trade has not been reciprocal. Between 1988 and 1991, Africa imported US$769 million worth of books from the European Community (EC); during the same time period the EC imports of books from Africa amounted to US$17.7 million (Roelofsen & Kohlmann, 1993).

Publishing capacity, and therefore the availability of children's books, is related to the extent of nationalization of the industry. Further criteria that might be used to classify the strength of a country's publishing capacity include statistics on population, literacy levels, income distribution, education and training systems, transportation and communication infrastructures, and government policies. The existence and diversity of local and regional publishers, printers, and traders and the condition of physical infrastructures also would need to be ascertained. The following is a fairly arbitrary classification of publishing capacity in some African countries based on these criteria:

Undeveloped	Weak	Moderate	Strong
Burkina Faso	Ethiopia	Kenya	South Africa
Guinea	Tanzania	Nigeria	
Uganda	Zambia	Zimbabwe	

Gathering and analyzing such information in each country would assist in determining where books can be obtained in the short term and what strategies are needed for the long term to ensure that there is a continuous book supply. The United Nations Educational, Scientific and Cultural Organization (UNESCO) is currently studying models for a global proposal to prepare national "book sector outlines"—succinct, pertinent, and updated information files profiling a nation's publishing activities, capacities, weaknesses, and achievements. The objective of the files is to facilitate publishers to solve problems by sharing experiences and assist donors to avoid duplication and waste in funds and efforts.

Publishing needs competition to thrive. Like most industries, it adheres to certain guiding principles that allow it to exist, grow, and flourish. Incorporation of these principles within program design can contribute substantially to the chances of establishing a sustainable book supply. Following are several of the more important of these guiding principles:

- The publisher is the architect of the book, responsible for a process that starts with research and financing and ends with selling the finished product. Much of the publisher's job lies in the successful marketing and distribution of books.
- Subsidizing production hurts competition, whereas subsidizing market demand strengthens competition.

- Trading books and copyrights, and other related publishing activities, must be conducted at a regional level because many local markets in Africa are too small to sustain viable book industries and lack the required level of infrastructure.

- Publishers in the private sector must have access to the profitable textbook market in order to publish the higher risk supplementary books that can contribute to the development of the lifetime reading habit.

- Publishers must have access to capital in the form of commercial credit.

"Book Famine" in Africa: Perception or Reality?

The term "book famine" has been used to describe aptly the book situation in Africa. It is accurate because it correctly conveys the notion of extreme scarcity; it is functional because it has forced people to become aware of the problem. However, it has portrayed an entire continent as being helpless and hopeless. Similarly, each book sector study conducted in Africa recently by the World Bank has correctly described the scarcity of books in a particular country, but it has rarely conveyed the potential that exists in the publishing industry. Consequently, the reaction from donor countries has often been to advocate relief rather than development because it has been perceived that Africans may never be able to address their own book needs. However, there have been some promising developments in the publishing industry in African countries, and many countries studied show evidence of successful efforts in promoting local publishing capacity.

Promising Developments in African Publishing

African Publishers' Network

The *Development Directory of Indigenous Publishing* (Priestley, 1995) provides the complete names and addresses of approximately 200 major book publishers in Africa. *The African Book Publishing Record*, published bimonthly, gives bibliographic listings of new and forthcoming African publications and is compiled in collaboration with more than 800

African publishers, institutions, and associations. In fact, about 1,200 African publishers have developed extensive publishing programs over time. Many of these same publishers joined in 1992 to form the African Publishers' Network (APNET), which boasts 22 national publishers' associations as members. APNET's newsletter, the *African Publishing Review*, is distributed to 1,100 publishers in more than 40 countries. APNET also coordinates the first pan-African publishing training program and has been instrumental in making the Zimbabwe International Book Fair the continent's premier book event.

African Books Collective

The African Books Collective (ABC), a self-help initiative owned by 37 African publishers in 12 countries and based in Oxford, England, promotes and distributes members' books in Europe and North America. The stock inventory of ABC titles available for immediate supply is more than 1,000 titles. ABC has experienced a growth rate of 87% since its inception in 1990 and has been successful in attracting 500 library accounts and 300 trade accounts in a total of 48 countries on 5 continents (Priestley, 1993).

Regional Cooperation

The intra-African book trade, although in its infancy, has the potential to service Africa's book demands and to strengthen the private publisher. A 1993 meeting of buyers and sellers for the African publishing and printing industry (reported by Roelofsen & Kohlmann, 1993) underlined this potential in a practical way. By the end of the event, book orders worth US$200,000 had been confirmed, and orders for another US$2 million were under negotiation. However, the report on the meeting also noted that, in spite of the existence of large capacity in the African publishing and printing industry, the region relied heavily on the supply of books and other printed material from outside Africa: from 1988 to 1990 more than US$550 million of printed matter was imported annually. It was concluded in the meeting that joint ventures with African concerns in international tender procedures for book and printed matter provision should be encouraged, and it was recommended that book supply from Africa or with an African partner be given priority in tendering for the provision of products and services supported by development funds.

Case Studies in African Publishing Efforts

The following case studies provide evidence of a vibrant publishing industry in Africa. They are drawn from traditionally active publishing countries such as Kenya, Nigeria, Zimbabwe, and South Africa and also from Ghana and Tanzania, where only rudimentary publishing infrastructures exist.

Kenya

Kenya, with a moderately developed industry, provides an example of how multinational publishing companies (referred to as transnationals) that make a commitment to African publishing can, without much government interference, play a positive role in book development. [The governments of Nigeria and Zimbabwe also exercise few constraints on transnational publishing enterprises (Hill, 1992).]

The publishing industry in Kenya suffered dramatic losses in the 1970s when the local market stagnated due to economic uncertainty following Kenyatta's death. The closing of the Tanzanian border cut export trade, which resulted in the loss of up to 30% of the publishers' turnover. Transnationals pulled out or cut back their investment, state-run publishers stopped publishing because of the losses they were suffering, and at least eight local firms closed.

In 1985 primary, secondary, and university education were organized into eight-, four-, and four-year cycles, respectively. The reorganization required the speedy development and production of new teaching materials. In the private publishing sector, initial optimism about this project faded when attempts were made to monopolize textbook supply under the nation's two state publishers. However, at the same time the government abandoned state distribution of textbooks to the retail trade, putting acquisition decisions in the hands of teachers and allowing the number of bookshops in the country to double (from 200 to 400) between 1985 and 1989. Once textbooks were sold on the basis of merit, private publishers were able to profit from the lucrative trade that resulted. With the introduction of the new education system, the number of book titles published increased from 109 (including 55 text-books) in 1985 to 294 (including 191 textbooks) in 1989 (Chakava, 1992).

Close to 90% of Kenya's book business involves textbooks, and without access to this market few publishers can survive. An entire company frequently depends financially on a single textbook series it has published—one that is sold year after year, long after the initial development costs have been met. The profits allow the publisher to pursue another line of literature, children's books, or general books. Textbook series that have been longstanding and have contributed to publishers' profits include Oxford University Press Kenya's New Peak English Course series, East African Educational Publisher's Masome Ya Msingi series, and Longman Kenya's Msinga Wa Kiswahili series. It is the vitality of the textbook sector of the industry that has allowed the underdeveloped children's market to gain new attention and even new publishers. The increase in interest in this section of the market

Training a local workforce benefits the publishing industry and allows publishers to produce high-quality children's books in local languages for classroom use. © Scott Walter. Used by permission.

has been reflected in the founding of two associations, the Children's Literature Association of Kenya and the Council for the Promotion of Science Publications for Children in Africa (which organizes Nairobi's Pan-African Children's Book Fair).

The former Heinemann Kenya's situation is a good illustration of what can happen when a publishing company has the vision to train a local workforce. In 1970 Heinemann Kenya started publishing locally. By 1975 it was publishing 20 new titles a year, and it had launched the Spear Books imprint. By 1976 the company was entirely Kenyan run. In 1980, with the venture into primary school publishing, revenue from locally produced books exceeded that from imported books. Within six years, locally produced books represented 85% of the company's revenue. Through a public sale of shares, capital was raised to continue the localization of the company. By 1993 the company, now wholly owned by Kenyans, changed its name to East African Educational Publishers Ltd. The company continues to publish more than 40 titles per year including high-quality children's books.

The Kenyan publishing industry has also benefited from financial lenders located outside the country. Obtaining commercial credit is seldom possible for an industry considered high risk by Kenyan bankers. However, Sweden's Dag Hammarskjold Foundation manages a loan scheme to help Kenyan entrepreneurs strengthen the local publishing industry. The scheme will guarantee loans from Barclay's Bank of Kenya up to US$40,000 for establishing a new enterprise, expanding an existing one, or assisting the buy out of shares of a locally registered transnational publisher (Priestley, 1995).

Nigeria

Nigeria's book needs are massive. According to a former president of the Nigeria Publishers' Association, an estimated 250 million books per year are required for the country's 24 million students at all levels (Nwankwo, 1992). Although most books are currently printed in English, Nigeria's official language, future publishing efforts will have to cater to a diverse range of languages, notably Hausa, Igbo, and Yoruba.

At a time when it is clear that there is a need for a diverse local industry in Nigeria, the trend unfortunately seems to be in the opposite direction toward mass book importation. In 1989 the number of titles produced in Nigeria was 1,424, down from the 1984 figure of 1,836 titles (Nwankwo, 1992). This is an indication of lack of investment in the local industry—especially when it was estimated in 1984 that Nigeria imported 75% of all books sold (Orimalade, 1984, as cited in Rathgeber, 1992).

Nigeria's current publishing difficulties stem from the high cost of production materials, slow rate of sale, poor turnover of capital, lack of specialization, limited management resources, few reliable distribution agents and bookshops, a poor library network, and the near nonexistence of marketing data (Nwankwo, 1992).

Despite these problems Nigeria has the largest commercial publishing industry south of the Sahara with expertise in authorship, production, and distribution. It is not surprising, therefore, that the Nigerian Publishers' Association has been concerned with the impact of loans from the World Bank specifically in the area of book imports. In the words of one publisher, referring to the US$120 million loan secured by the Nigerian federal government for the book sector in 1991, "Massive importation of books without a commensurate attempt to encourage and stimulate local book production with a view to bridging future gaps in book supply to the school system can only spell doom to the local book industry and education" (Nwankwo, 1992, p. 166).

Zimbabwe

Zimbabwe boasts more than 30 active publishers, a strong publishers' association, a book development council, and the premier book event in Africa—the Zimbabwe International Book Fair. In 1991, the combined book output of the 24 indigenous publishing firms in the country in the nonformal education sector was greater than that of the transnational publishers.

The majority of Zimbabweans still do not have access to the book trade. Even in the urban townships, where almost 20% of the population lives, not a single bookshop exists to serve the book reading needs. In response to this situation, a progressive bookshop (Grassroots Books) created the Zimbabwe Book Marketing Scheme (ZBMS), which posed the question "Why do people not buy books?" In addition to the obvious economic reasons, ZBMS concluded that the primary reasons related to access, a lack of awareness of the importance and value of books, and a lack of knowledge of what types of books were published and where books were available.

ZBMS has approached the problem of domestic marketing in four ways, with varying degrees of success:

1. New distribution systems and markets were identified through mail-order service and the establishment of book clubs. The mail-order service receives orders for about 5,000 books annually. The book clubs are based on the principle of friends sharing the use and costs of books. By 1994, 44 clubs had been established in rural areas.

2. Information was disseminated through a quarterly newsletter that reported on all aspects of book promotion. Due to financial constraints, the newsletter ceased publication in 1994.

3. A "budding writers' competition" was administered and has since evolved into the writers' and readers' campaign. This traveling book sale, with author readings and group discussions, is an outreach program that seeks to make the book an event in both urban and rural areas.

4. A database of all books published in the region has been set up, which allows for better promotion and knowledge of the market.

South Africa

South Africa's publishing industry currently is being restructured with the intention of redressing historical divisions and pursuing a greater market share throughout the continent. A single publishers' association has been formed to unite the Publishers' Association of South Africa (PASA—formerly representing apartheid's status quo and the textbook industry) with the breakaway Independent Publishers' Association of South Africa (IPASA—the smaller "alternative houses"). This bigger, richer, and more technologically advanced South African industry could finally change the face of African publishing.

The "New South Africa" is both welcomed and feared by the AP-NET community because northward expansion will bring new opportunities for copublishing, training, and access to the lucrative South

African market while challenging APNET members' capacity to compete with the wealthier South Africans. Within South Africa there is also concern about the industry's ability to reflect the culture and aspirations of the majority population.

British transnationals have invested heavily in several of the IPASA publishing houses in order to expand their presence in the South African market and possibly throughout the entire continent. In 1993 the British transnational Macmillan was questioned by the IPASA director on the subject of reaching a deal with the governing African National Congress. IPASA issued the familiar warning that "any attempt to constitute a privileged relationship between any publishing house and the future state would be exceptionally prejudicial, if not fatal, to the interests of vibrant, independent, and indigenous publishing in South Africa" (Moss, as quoted in "Country Focus," 1993, p. 8). In 1994 Macmillan created a new company, Nolwazi, together with Thebe Investments Corporation (an ANC-linked company) and Skotaville Publishers. It will be interesting to watch the effect of this project, especially because the Director of Skotaville, Mothobi Mutloatse (1992), previously had argued that African writers must be published by African houses as an inevitable step in the process of African emancipation. Because textbooks mean survival for a South African publisher, perhaps Mutloatse simply decided to be pragmatic and accept the necessity of capital investment from Macmillan.

Ghana

Ghana's efforts to put books into the school system followed a pattern that was established across much of the continent. Following independence in 1957, textbooks were provided at no cost to parents under a government-run publishing scheme. Over time, parents and other potential buyers came to perceive books as goods provided by someone else; they were not goods to which a monetary value had been attached. The "free" book scheme determined that there would be no book trade, no bookshops, and no private sector publishers. Predictably, the supply of books was short lived as government budgets became smaller and state publishing houses were cut back. Despite the best of intentions, in time, Ghana became virtually a bookless society.

Following an overhaul of the education system, the government decided to introduce a new curriculum and new textbooks. However, publishers were given only 120 days to deliver the texts (from the time the contract was signed to completion of printing) (Dekutsey, 1993). Because local publishing operations had stagnated, they were in no position to compete with the United Kingdom transnationals for this lucrative market.

Problems quickly emerged because of the decision to introduce a new curriculum and new texts. Entire print runs had been earmarked by the Ghana Ministry of Education. It became apparent that, despite a large textbook infusion, the demand for books did not cease; in fact, it had only begun. The supply was inadequate. No provision was made for demand by individual purchasers, normally parents. To resolve this dilemma, the Ministry, which had kept copyright for the textbooks, contracted four local publishers to produce reprints for commercial sale. Although the four publishers still continue to derive income from this arrangement, the benefit is less than it would been had they been brought in on copublishing schemes with the transnationals from the beginning.

Within Ghana's publishing sector there is abundant evidence of vitality. The publishers' association has established its own secretariat, supported the creation of APNET, compiled an excellent catalog of members' publications, and run numerous up-country (areas of Africa that are not near the major urban center) and national book fairs. In addition to marketing textbooks, younger firms in particular are starting to branch out in other lines such as children's books, preschool children's material, and adult fiction.

Tanzania

Tanzania, like Ghana, has experienced problems associated with state monopolies, book importations, and a lack of investment in local firms. The country also is one of the poorest in Africa and is struggling to repair its collapsed economy. Since 1991 Tanzania publishers have been reversing the decline in publishing output by successfully subscribing to the strategy of the Children's Book Project (CBP). Operating as an independent structure and funded by the Danish, Dutch, and Canadian governments, the CBP has advanced the publication of more than 50 new children's titles in Swahili by acting as a market force.

The CBP strategy represents an unconventional use of a subsidy. Publishers are first invited to submit manuscripts; then a board, comprising Tanzanian teachers, child welfare experts, and children, selects the best manuscripts (15 in the first year, 80 by the fifth year) for purchase. Publishers do not receive an actual subsidy for bringing these manuscripts to publication; however, the project is committed to buying 3,000 copies at 35% below the retail price (the discount given to any bulk buyer), which covers production costs but does not allow for profits. The project distributes the 3,000 copies to up-country rural and school libraries that have such limited funds that there is no danger of undermining the publishers' sales. Publishers are also required to print, market, and distribute at least an additional 2,000 copies. It is in the successful sale of these additional 2,000 books that the publisher makes a profit.

The sustainability of this project is based on reactivating the book trade. By introducing books to a new generation of readers and by ensuring access to books through libraries and bookshops, it is hoped that the reading habit will grow, the potential book market will expand, and ultimately publishers will meet the increased demand. The key is to stimulate the book trade's vitality by allowing textbook publishers to enter the market on a commercial basis. The December 1994 announcement that government-owned Tanzania Publishing House was to be privatized seemed to recognize this point.

The CBP is currently being studied by the project's donors with a view to expansion to other countries.

The Way Forward

Progress cannot be made in promoting children's book publishing in Africa if funding is directed to a particular goal in isolation or in ignorance of the entire publishing process in any given country or region. Armed with a thorough knowledge of the local publishing context, and working with local publishers and officials, assistance for children's publications should consider the following features.

Develop Indigenous Publishing Capacity

Getting the industry moving is the top priority. This includes getting writers writing, editors editing, and booksellers selling. These are skill-based professions, and if a trained and competent workforce is to be established, the opportunity must be given to trainees to develop their chosen craft. The reform agenda should focus on the production of a maximum variety of titles and small print runs. This will allow those involved in the process to gain experience and learn from small mistakes rather than large ones. Aiming to publish a few titles with massive print runs does not give the variety necessary to grab and retain readers' attention, and it limits the potential for those involved to gain experience in the various aspects of publishing. If sustainability is to be a major objective, putting books into every child's hands cannot be the immediate priority. For most of Africa, this can be achieved only through large-scale importation schemes and supply sustained through many loans. The priority should be to develop the publishing industry so that it eventually has the capacity to put books into every child's hands.

Subsidize Purchasing Power Rather Than Production

When asked what assistance they would appreciate, publishers are likely to answer, "Buy my books." Normally they do not want someone else to do the work for them; they require an expanding market. For them, the two greatest handicaps have always been the shortage of capital and the high level of risk in the industry. If a scheme for book purchases, such as the Children's Book Project in Tanzania, is established for schools or libraries, the publisher is likely to react positively, secure in the knowledge that a guaranteed purchase minimizes risk and provides ready income capital. Competition with other publishers will still exist; a certain percentage of the books will have to be sold outside the project in the marketplace. Quality is thus encouraged by competition. Subsidizing production on the other hand does not necessarily guarantee performance because the funding is disbursed before the product is complete. To make initial funds available, the donor should explore the possibilities of loan guarantees.

Create a Demand for Children's Literature

Demand is a function of availability, cost, and product appeal. It will be difficult for wholesalers and retailers to expand operations if denied access to the textbook market due to government monopoly. In Kenya, after the government abandoned textbook distribution, 200 new bookshops opened. An increase in outlets usually means greater sales opportunities, larger print runs, and less expensive books. A scheme of directed purchases can contribute to consumer demand for books, particularly if publishers are required to market a certain percentage of the print run beyond that covered by the guaranteed purchase. In attempting to cater to the market and increase production standards, publishers will face a number of difficult choices; for instance, they must decide if they wish to produce a relatively inexpensive product and forgo color printing or maximize the visual impact of the book through use of color.

Promote Books

Assistance in the form of donor aid or national grants to children's publishing should endorse book promotion. A program can be implemented through a publishers' association or a book development council and can be designed to encourage the book reading habit by improving book accessibility and by lowering prices. Funds would support book fairs and publishers' promotions. The scheme would strive to increase sales by establishing mail-order distribution systems and book clubs and by supporting book exports and the establishment of bookshops. The Zimbabwe Book Marketing Scheme represents a good example of such a project.

Diversify Publishing

No one publisher can produce the variety of titles that society needs. A publishing initiative should create an environment that encourages new publishers and rewards only those who perform well. Transnational publishers can contribute to the diversification process, but care should be taken to ensure that their greater resources and access to capital should not enable them to overwhelm the market. Their commitment to building the national publishing industry can be demonstrated in the establishment of business partnerships between publishers from developed and developing countries. Copublishing arrangements have numerous benefits including the potential they offer for inservice training, lower development costs for both sides, and access to new markets.

Promote Indigenous Publications

Children should have access to literature written in a familiar language, which brings them in contact with their own culture, lifestyle, sports, and heroes. Local authors are best equipped to introduce young readers to these important sources of information and pleasure. It is equally true that stories frequently cut across cultural boundaries constituting an international literature with universal appeal. Schemes to copublish internationally popular children's books in the developing world can play an important role in fostering the reading habit. Such schemes need not, and indeed should not, thrive at the expense of the production of local manuscripts. Copublishing with other regional publishers could be an excellent solution to examine first. The supply of manuscripts also can be encouraged through writers' competitions.

Support Training

Training must be provided to improve the industry and secure its future. Editorial and design skills tend to be in short supply within African publishing houses as are the skills needed for book marketing and selling. Publishing is not an exact science and is difficult to teach and master in a classroom setting. The "sixth sense" that a publisher must develop—the instinct that tells what will work and what will not in a particular situation—is best acquired through apprenticeship with an experienced professional working within the same environment. Ideally, an employee of one publishing house would be assigned to a more active house for four to six months. Short-term workshops with outside expertise are likely to be effective if the content is focused on specific needs such as improving design or composition. Training costs should be at least partially shared by the benefiting publishing house and not paid solely by the donor. This should increase the likelihood that merit and potential would influence a publisher's nominations for training. Training solutions involving international publishers not only may be effective but can also offer long-term mutual benefits through business arrangements embracing copublishing, adaptations, and sale of rights. This may in turn open new markets and possibly lead to injections of new capital for small publishing enterprises.

Direct Support to Libraries

A government committed to the development of the independent reading habit among its youth must have a library support program. Libraries offer access to books, in particular, for those who cannot afford to buy them. Libraries provide ongoing, long-term markets for publishers as well. Although library requirements may vary from city to village, overall libraries need a great variety of titles. Provided they have adequate purchasing power, libraries offer one of the most reliable supports for the publishing industry. The mechanism used by the Norwegian government might be replicated to good effect in developing countries: the library system purchases 1,000 copies of all titles published each year.

Final Comments

If individuals, institutions, and governments recognize the value of literacy and the need to have a population that not only *can* read but *will* read, they must be willing to commit scarce resources toward the acquisition of books. The concept of the free book must be rejected. Distribution schemes in which all costs are absorbed by the government are unlikely to be sustainable in the long run. They create a false notion of real costs and destroy rather than develop the market (see also Chapter 9). Instead of donating books, governments might be better advised to allocate budgets for schools to make their own purchases. This has the double impact of enticing the bookseller up-country and allowing the consumer to select the books. Accountability by those handling the funds would be crucial, but a system of credits not unlike that currently used in Zimbabwe is feasible.

The development of a literate environment is a process that spans generations. There is no quick or easy solution, and any emergency book supply program implemented in isolation of local and regional publishing will never have the desired impact. In contrast to other industries, publishers do not typically seek massive solutions to massive problems; sensibly they tend to seek slow sustained growth, starting small and expanding a project only after some measure of success has been attained. The independent African publishers have understood this and have pursued this approach with a tenacious attitude to survival.

Aid should take the form of lead funding and should promote initiative in the publishing sector. Rather than serve as a disincentive, it should foster the development of higher levels of performance from the entire industry. The challenge for the African publishing industry is to strive for enhanced performance, assume new targets and responsibilities, and welcome competition, all in service to the reader.

References

Chakava, H. (1992). Kenyan publishing: Independence and dependence. In P.G. Altbach (Ed.), *Publishing and development in the third world* (pp. 119–150). London: Hans Zell.

Country focus. (1993). *African Publishing Review*, 2,(4), 8.

Dekutsey, W. (1993). Ghana: A case study in publishing development. LOGOS, 4(2), 62–72.

Hill, A. (1992). British publishers' contribution to African literature. LOGOS, 3(1), 45–52.

Mutloatse, M. (1992). Indigenous publishing in South Africa: The case of Skotaville Publishers. In P.G. Altbach (Ed.), *Publishing and development in the third world* (pp. 211–222). London: Hans Zell.

Nwankwo, V. (1992). Publishing in Nigeria today. In P.G. Altbach (Ed.), *Publishing and development in the third world* (pp. 156–168). London: Hans Zell.

Priestley, C. (1993). *Book and publishing assistance programmes: A review and inventory* (Bellagio Studies in Publishing No. 2). Bellagio Publishing Network Research and Information Centre. Buffalo, NY: State University of New York at Buffalo.

Priestley, C. (Compiler). (1995). *Development directory of indigenous publishing*. Harare, Zimbabwe: African Publishers' Network.

Rathgeber, E. (1992). African book publishing: Lessons from the 1980's. In P.G. Altbach (Ed.), *Publishing and development in the third world*. London: Hans Zell.

Roelofsen, H.G., & Kohlmann, R.J. (1993, June 15). *Promotion of Intra-African trade: Buyers/sellers meeting for the African publishing and printing industry* (held in Grand-Baie, Mauritius, May 10–14). Report prepared for the United Nations Conference on Trade and Development/General Agreement on Tariffs and Trade International Trade Centre (Project No. RAF/47/51).

8 | Using Book Floods to Raise Literacy Levels in Developing Countries

Warwick B. Elley

A 1990 WORLD BANK report on education and development (Haddad et al., 1990) highlights the value of educational investment and the need for more attention to the quality of basic education in developing countries. Having worked extensively in several of developing countries, I have become increasingly optimistic about the benefits of both these strategies. Raising literacy levels pays off. Once people can read, they not only expand their horizons and increase their confidence, but they also have the potential to acquire useful knowledge independently—knowledge about better nutrition, childrearing, health, government policies, farming, and many vocational skills. However, achieving better quality education in poor countries, where underqualified teachers teach oversized classes in underresourced classrooms, is not easy.

In the past, educators have initiated campaigns or programs to improve basic education that have provided resources for teacher training and retraining, curriculum reform, textbook provision, educational television, model or "beacon" schools, radios in schools, and many other reform strategies. Some of these approaches have been successful, but most are slow, expensive, and dependent on progress in many other areas.

There is one initiative that has received too little attention, and yet it is one that has worked effectively in several developing countries.

It has worked in various South Pacific Islands, Singapore, the Middle East, and other parts of the world where children acquire their schooling in a language different from that of the home, which is a very common situation in the schools of Africa, Asia, and the South Pacific. The formula is to immerse children in a flood of high-interest illustrated storybooks in the target language—and ensure that the children read them. The "book flood" approach has been tried in the rural primary schools of Fiji, with hundreds of Indian and Fijian students, and has shown dramatic improvements in reading, writing, listening, vocabulary, and grammar (Elley & Mangubhai, 1983). It has worked in Singapore, where children who spoke Chinese, Malay, or Tamil at home learned to read and write fluently in English during the first three years of their schooling (Elley, 1991; Ng, 1987). Formal evaluations of Singapore student achievement and teacher support have been consistently positive. The Singapore initiative has since become a national program, with positive results, as evidenced by the high literacy rate shown by Singapore students in the 1991 International Association for the Evaluation of Educational Achievement Study of Reading Literacy (Elley, 1992; see also Chapter 2) in addition to the formal evaluations of the program.

The book flood approach has been tried with positive impact in Niue (in the South Pacific), where grade three Niuean children learned to read in English with a set of high-interest storybooks that stressed local themes, humor, and popular storylines (Elley, 1980). It also produced impressive results with Hispanic students in Arizona in the United States (Schon, Hopkins, & Davis, 1982), with Pakistani students in England (Hafiz & Tudor, 1989), with French Canadian students in New Brunswick (Lightbown, 1989), in modified form with Israeli students in Israel (Feitelson, Kita, & Goldstein, 1986), and with kindergarten children in Israel learning modern literary Arabic (Feitelson, Goldstein, Iraqi, & Share, 1993). (These programs will be explained in a later section.)

Rationale for Book Floods

What is the rationale for using a book flood approach to raise literacy levels? The principles underpinning this approach are as follows.

- *Immersion in large quantities of meaningful text.* This is a necessary element in acquiring literacy in any language. A traditional focus on drills and skills fragments the language and sends the wrong messages to children about the functions of print and books. Regular encounters with meaningful text are more productive than a focus on form and structure (Krashen, 1982).

- *Incidental language learning.* Children learn most of their vocabulary and language structures incidentally from reading and listening rather than from systematic, teacher-directed "block-building" approaches (Elley, 1989; Nagy, Herman, & Anderson, 1985).

- *Integration of oral and written language.* Discussion and writing about an interesting story or experience enables students to transfer what they are learning, with interest, from one mode (reading) to another (speaking and writing).

- *High intrinsic motivation.* When children listen to or read a gripping story that contains elements of novelty, surprise, humor, or other "collative variables" (Berlyne, 1960), they are more likely to concentrate harder and learn faster than when they work only to obey the teacher or pass an examination. A genuine desire to find out what happens in a story is a key incentive to focus a child's mind. Good quality children's literature has the potential to hook children on books.

- *Easy implementation.* A book flood policy does not require extensive teacher training or repeated persuasion of teachers to implement it. In the South Pacific programs, teachers with modest levels of education acquired the necessary skills in a few days; most implemented the program readily and were quickly persuaded by its merits.

What Specifically Does a Book Flood Entail?

Not all book floods have adopted the same methods, but the majority have followed some adaptation of this formula:

- *Start young.* The programs are usually targeted at elementary school children when they are learning to read in the national language. Experiments at the secondary level have usually been less dramatic in their impact.

- *Use many books.* A large stock of high-interest books is provided (in small installments). In Fiji, the rural schools were given approximately 250 books per classroom over two years; in Singapore about 150 books were provided; in Niue the number was only about 50. Policies of sharing books among classrooms and making new books (with parent help) can supplement these stocks.

- *Choose books judiciously.* The books are selected with an eye to student interest, illustrations, local themes, sensitivity to cultural differences, predictability of language, print size, potential for new language acquisition, durability, and cost. Standard written exercises at the end of each chapter are not recommended. Providing multiple copies of a few favorite stories is a sensible policy.

- *Use shared reading methods.* Teachers are trained to use the shared reading method. This training may take two or three sessions, with follow-up visits to schools. With the shared reading method, after initial class discussion of a chosen book, its cover, and prediction of contents, the teacher reads the story to the children as they sit around him or her on the floor following the words in the book. It helps to have books with very large print. During the reading, there are occasional pauses for discussion, explanation, prediction of the story, or vocabulary instruction, but not enough to lose interest. Children may then discuss or draw pictures to illustrate parts of the story. The next day the story is reread, with children joining in where they can. The story may be read several times during the next week or two, until most children can read it aloud—in unison. Individuals or groups may take different parts; the story may be acted, adapted, rewritten by the children, or converted by the children into a large "blown-up" book, with pictures and large print. During the reading, the teacher will draw attention to parts of the text for incidental study—vocabulary, grammar, punctuation, a clever turn of phrase, or other element. Such teaching takes place at the point of interest and is relevant to the theme. If children become bored, another story is presented.

- *Encourage children to read often.* Teachers should also allow time for "uninterrupted sustained silent reading" or "drop everything and read." In such approaches, children read silently for enjoyment from self-selected books for 15 to 20 minutes each day. Teachers also may display, promote, talk about, and read aloud selections from the books. Regular, recreational reading aloud by the teacher is a feature of most of the successful projects, and some advice and practice at story reading is important during project implementation if teachers are unaccustomed to the method. No written exercises on comprehension are given to the class; children will sometimes talk briefly to their group (or the teacher) about books they enjoyed.

How Strong Is the Evidence for the Effectiveness of Book Floods?

In a report (Elley, 1991) on the evaluation of nine book-based programs, all showed a marked positive impact—some of them dramatic. One particular project that has provided a model for policy in Singapore and in the South Pacific was the Fiji Book Flood, which is summarized in the following section.

Fiji Book Flood

Twelve rural schools were chosen for the Fiji Book Flood project, eight for the book flood and four for control schools. After pretesting, the schools were matched for reading achievement levels, age, ethnic composition, and experience of teachers. The project started at grades four and five (ages 10 to 11 years) and continued for two years (1980 and 1981). More than 500 students and 25 teachers were involved.

Half of the teachers in the book flood schools were trained in a three-day inservice course to implement the shared reading method; the other half followed the silent reading approach, with occasional story reading aloud by the teacher, and had no special inservice training. The control group teachers had a one-day workshop designed to improve their skills in the implementation of their structured audiolingual language program. This program had been taught in almost all South Pacific schools for at least 10 years, and was designed to

One of the methods used in a book flood program is frequent silent reading. © READ Educational Trust, South Africa. Used by permission.

give students repeated oral practice with the correct grammatical forms and structures of English before they used them in reading and writing. It was a program promoted by all governments and marketed by the South Pacific Commission, an international body designed to improve the social and economic conditions of the region.

Teachers in the eight book flood schools were given 250 books, in sets of about 50, over two years. Funds were raised from charities, and the books were purchased from New Zealand, the United States, and the United Kingdom because there was very little indigenous children's literature in Fiji. Books were kept inside the classrooms in book corners, classroom libraries, or on display. (See Table 1 for an overview of the design of the Fiji Book Flood.)

Time spent on teaching English language arts—reading, writing, grammar, and so forth—was standardized. The researchers visited the schools about every two months to ensure that teachers were administering the program as intended, and to observe lessons and students' work.

Table 1   Design of Fiji Book Flood

	Program Year 1980				Program Year 1981
	February	March	April–October	November	November
Shared reading method group (4 schools)	pretests	three-day workshop	250 books supplied to grades 4 & 5	posttests	follow-up tests
Silent reading method group (4 schools)	pretests	no workshop	250 books supplied to grades 4 & 5	posttests	follow-up tests
Control group (4 schools)	pretests	one-day workshop	SPC/Tate Audio-Lingual Programme no extra books	posttests	follow-up tests

At the end of two years, all students were tested by outside educators on standard tests of reading, listening, writing, vocabulary, and grammar. Students' results on the national Fiji Intermediate Examination, administered in grade six by the Fiji Ministry of Education, were also recorded. The results of the evaluation were consistent and striking. After one year, the two book flood groups (shared reading and silent reading) had gained in reading comprehension ability at twice the normal rate of growth. They were also well ahead of the control groups in each test of reading, listening, and grammar, in both grade levels four and five (see Figure 1), but the differences were not significant in the test of oral language. After two years, when similar tests were applied, the gains had increased in all language areas (see Table 2). The results on the Fiji Intermediate Examination were also positive: the shared reading group doubled their usual pass rate in English, so that twice as many children that year left their villages to attend high school in town. One of the small schools in the program had the second highest performance level in Fiji.

Class-by-class analyses showed that the teachers whose students gained the most were those who followed the shared reading program as intended and those in the silent reading groups who read stories aloud most often. One teacher could not be persuaded to continue with the shared reading program, and his students' test results were very low. By contrast, the one teacher in the control groups whose students scored above average was a teacher who was reading aloud to her class daily, from her personal library of storybooks. This was an unusual practice in these schools at the time, and the researchers were unaware of this teacher's instructional method.

To illustrate the difference between the experimental and control groups after two years, samples of the children's writing style are presented. At the end of grade six, students were asked to write about a sequence of four pictures showing the story of a fire in a Fijian village. The modal score given to the shared reading group on this task was 9 out of 10. Sample openings of two stories with this score were as follows:

> "One morning when Luke's mother was washing, and the men were drinking yaqona, Luke was boiling the water."

> "One day, Tomasi's mother was washing clothes beside the river, Tomasi's father was drinking yaqona under a shady tree, Tomasi was cooking the food beside their house, and his brother was carrying buckets of water...."

Figure 1   Mean Percentage Scores on Posttests for Fiji Book Flood—First Year

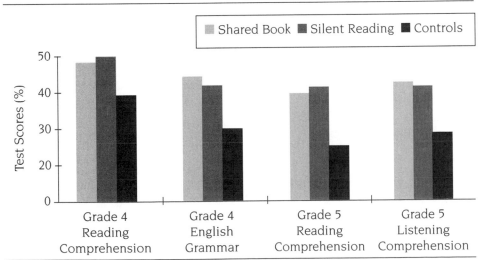

Table 2 Residual Mean Scores* on Tests for Three Programs in Fiji Book Flood (1981 and 1982)

	(1) Shared Reading		(2) Silent Reading		(3) Control Group		(1) + (2) v (3)
	N	RM	N	RM	N	RM	F tests
Grade 4 (1980)							
RC	75	0.59	84	1.21	106	−1.40	17.70**
ES	71	0.99	84	0.63	106	−0.95	10.90**
WR	37	2.08	43	−0.35	54	−1.33	1.06
OL	34	1.56	38	−0.68	49	−0.71	2.60
Grade 5 (1980)							
RC	91	2.08	88	−0.14	91	−1.82	21.07**
LC	91	4.31	87	0.63	91	−2.13	35.74**
ES	91	3.14	87	0.24	91	−0.33	0.83
WC	91	1.51	87	1.40	91	−0.07	1.01
Grade 5 (1981)							
RC	66	2.13	70	2.67	91	−3.60	58.14**
LC	66	1.10	70	0.81	91	−1.45	28.73**
ES	66	0.81	70	1.28	91	−1.55	27.49**
Total	66	4.02	70	4.78	91	−6.59	55.29**
Grade 6 (1981)							
RC	81	1.27	64	1.40	87	−2.22	24.66**
VK	81	0.92	64	1.62	87	−2.02	30.17**
ES	81	1.65	64	1.22	87	−2.46	24.73**
WC	81	0.52	64	0.66	87	−0.99	25.00**
Total	81	4.35	64	4.89	87	−7.64	37.96**

N = number; RM = residual mean; RC = reading comprehension; ES = English structures; WR = word recognition; OL = oral language; LC = listening comprehension; WC = written composition; VK = vocabulary knowledge.
* The residual scores were calculated by conducting a regression analysis using pretest scores to predict posttest scores for the whole sample. Residual scores represent the deviation between actual and predicted scores.
**$p < .001$
From "Acquiring Literacy in a Second Language: The Effect of Book-Based Programs," by W.B. Elley, 1991, *Language Learning*, 41, p. 387.

By contrast, the modal score for this task in the control group was 2 out of 10. The compositions in this group usually had at least 12 grammatical or spelling mistakes in the first 15 lines; they showed no fluency or sense in the sentences, and the story was often incoherent. Three examples (given a score of 2) from the control group were as follows:

> "Is ther was the women in the tree. mothe sitg in the tree there was a looking at hes mother...."

> "One day there boy Seru is make the tea to drinking his morth was the colth...."

> "One day morning their were a house any village by the sea...."

Encouraging results had occurred after two years in the Fiji Book Flood program. In the first year, the impact was most obvious in English reading and listening tests. In the second year, the benefits were clearly seen in writing and vocabulary; and on the national examination they were also apparent in science, social studies, and even the vernacular language (Fijian). It is interesting to note that the benefits were reflected with similar impact in both multiple-choice and open-ended test items.

The Singapore REAP Program

Reports on the Fiji Book Flood have been influential in changing policy in Singapore, where the government was concerned about low English standards in primary schools. After pilot studies in schools during 1984 and 1985, the Reading and English Acquisition Program (REAP) was developed (Kee, 1984; Ng, 1987), based on extensive book floods with shared reading and language experience methods. (REAP is also discussed in Chapters 2 and 3.) The program was taught in grades one to three and was found to produce consistently good results. In a succession of highly controlled comparisons between experimental and control groups between 1985 and 1988, researchers found significant differences favoring REAP in 53 out of 65 language test comparisons (Elley, 1991; Ng, 1987). The teachers—who were initially skeptical of a philosophy based on students' interest and fiction books—gave it whole-hearted support when they saw it in action, and even more so when the impact was shown in improved examination results. After the evaluations were reported to the government, the Ministry of Education nationalized the program in 1987, as mentioned. Since then, the International Association for the Evaluation of Educational Achievement Study of Reading Literacy results have shown that Singapore students are among the best readers (Elley, 1992).

Book Floods in Other Areas

The "Fiafia" book program introduced to third-grade children on the island of Niue led to marked improvements in reading comprehension, word recognition, and oral language after one year. The Fiafia program (De'Ath, 1980) is based on using 48 locally produced storybooks, with indigenous themes, illustrations, and humor. The teachers were trained briefly to use the shared book method, and many used it effectively, as indicated by observations and by the impressive test gains.

A book flood in Spanish was conducted in Tempe, Arizona (Schon, Hopkins, & Davis, 1982), with 49 Hispanic 7- to 9-year-olds in four elementary schools. After eight months, these children showed superior gains in Spanish reading comprehension, vocabulary, reading speed, and attitudes, at no cost to their English language achievement.

Supporting evidence comes also from a study of Pakistani English as a second language students in the United Kingdom, who read silently from self-selected books in daily one-hour sessions. Significant gains were registered after only 12 weeks in reading comprehension, vocabulary, and writing (Hafiz & Tudor, 1989).

In a Canadian study (Lightbown, 1989), Francophone 8- to 10-year-olds in New Brunswick read daily from a wide variety of English books, while listening to tape recordings of the text. No deliberate teaching or discussion took place in these sessions, yet they proved more effective than the current aural-oral programs, which involve formal dialogues, songs, and minimal reading practice. They also were more popular with the children.

Feitelson has conducted two studies in Israel to investigate the impact of daily story reading to 5- and 6-year-olds—one study with Hebrew children and one with Arab children both learning Arabic (Feitelson, Goldstein, Iraqi, & Share, 1993; Feitelson, Kita, & Goldstein, 1986). Again, the results showed strong positive results across a wide range of language tests.

In addition, studies conducted on children learning literacy in their first language confirm the benefits of reading widely. After reviewing a range of studies of first-language learning in many countries using regular sustained reading practices, Krashen (1989) concluded that much evidence supports the view that language is best learned by regular reading: "Large quantities of light, 'low risk' reading, in which students are not held responsible for content, in which they can skip words without fear of missing anything...will result in vocabulary growth and overall language competence" (p. 455). Krashen noted too that the students studied achieved at higher levels in both multiple-choice and free-response tests, a finding that was supported by the Fiji Book Flood.

Concluding Remarks

There is still more to learn about the impact of book floods. Follow-up studies have confirmed predictions that children do learn a great deal of new vocabulary from context, just from listening to interesting stories read aloud (Elley, 1989). However, when interest levels drop, the benefits are not so apparent. As an empirical researcher, I now have data to support the recommendations of literature enthusiasts that suggest there are many potential benefits in a good book, provided it grasps and holds students' interest. Not only do students expand their language by reading widely, they also learn much about other times and places, stimulate their imagination, gain insights into human nature, are able to follow their specific interests and hobbies, and enjoy an escape from unpleasant realities. And once children learn to appreciate books, they will read more often and improve their skills. In an era when so many activities compete for children's leisure time, we cannot expect that a lasting interest in reading will overcome all obstacles; but if students do not enjoy reading, they are never likely to make a habit of it.

Evidence has shown that book floods do have clear advantages in raising literacy levels in the schools of developing countries, where children are learning in a language different from their home. The book flood method

- requires less teacher training than most methods;
- shows consistent and dramatic effects on reading and other language skills;

- generates enthusiasm and positive attitudes in teachers and students;
- produces effects that transfer to other subjects;
- assists teachers whose competence in the target language is limited by providing them with good language models; and
- is easy to justify to local governments because it increases the resources provided to schools.

The main disadvantages of the book flood approach are the costs of the books and the logistical problems involved in selecting and distributing them. The optimal time for using this method is the beginning grades, in which students are switching to the target language. In most cases this has been English, but the principles should apply to any other language in which there is a wealth of good children's books available.

As Oliveira stressed in Chapter 4, the costs of providing trade books that appeal to primary school children are often considerable. And, although these costs are somewhat less than those of typical textbooks, a larger number of trade books are required for students. However, it is possible that costs could be substantially reduced with bulk purchases or under a policy of sharing between schools or classes within schools. Compared with typical costs for new school textbooks, teaching aids, and accompanying teacher training, the costs of high-quality children's books are not necessarily excessive. For instance, in a recent book flood in Sri Lanka, the cost of books was kept to US$1.00 per book, or US$100.00 per class (Elley & Foster, 1996). Moreover, there is evidence that such funding would be worthwhile, that schools would have something to show for the expense, that the teachers and students would find a new enthusiasm for their learning, and that inroads could be made on the persistent intergenerational cycles of illiteracy in developing countries.

These benefits are substantial when compared with more traditional campaigns to increase the number of textbooks in schools. It is an unusual textbook that enthuses children to continue learning. Few children wish to read their textbook many times or to read the identical textbook of the other students in their class. A flood of 100 different books in a classroom, by contrast, provides a rich resource for many months of reading, by everyone. Of course, a set of textbooks for all students is more defensible in content areas—mathematics, science, and social studies—especially in later grades. However, the benefits of textbooks would be enhanced if they were provided *after* children have developed competence and confidence in their reading and writing—*after* they have been exposed to a variety of good books.

References

Berlyne, D.E. (1960). *Conflict, arousal and curiosity*. New York: McGraw-Hill.

De'Ath, P.R.T. (1980). The shared book experience and ESL. *Directions*, 4, 13–22.

Elley, W.B. (1980). A comparison of content-interest and structuralist reading programs in Niue primary schools. *New Zealand Journal of Educational Studies*, 15, 39–53.

Elley, W.D. (1989). Vocabulary acquisition from listening to stories. *Reading Research Quarterly*, 24, 174–187.

Elley, W.B. (1991). Acquiring literacy in a second language: The effect of book-based programs. *Language Learning*, 41, 375–411.

Elley, W.B. (1992). *How in the world do students read?* Hamburg, Germany: International Association for the Evaluation of Educational Achievement.

Elley, W.B., & Foster, D. (1996). *Books in schools project, Sri Lanka: Final report*. London: International Book Development.

Elley, W.B., & Mangubhai, F. (1983). The impact of reading on second language learning. *Reading Research Quarterly*, 19, 53–67.

Feitelson, D., Goldstein, Z., Iraqi, J., & Share, D.L. (1993). Effects of listening to story reading on aspects of literary acquisition in a diglossic situation. *Reading Research Quarterly*, 28, 70–79.

Feitelson, D., Kita, B., & Goldstein, Z. (1986). *Effect of reading series stories to first graders on their comprehension and use of language*. Haifa, Israel: University of Haifa.

Haddad, W.D., Carnoy, M., Rinaldi, R., & Regel, O. (1990). *Education and development: Evidence for new priorities* (World Bank Discussion Paper No. 95). Washington, DC: World Bank.

Hafiz, F.M., & Tudor, I. (1989). Extensive reading and the development of language skills. *English Language Teaching Journal*, 43, 4–11.

Kee, L. (1984). *Concept paper on REAP*. Singapore: Ministry of Education.

Krashen, S.D. (1982). *Principles and practice in second language acquisition*. New York: Pergamon.

Krashen, S.D. (1989). We acquire vocabulary and spelling by reading: Additional evidence for the input hypothesis. *Modern Language Journal*, 73, 440–465.

Lightbown, P.M. (1989). Can they do it themselves? A comprehension-based ESL course for young children. In R. Courchene, J. St. John, C. Therien, & J. Glidden

(Eds.), *Proceedings of the conference on comprehension-based second language teaching: Current trends*. Ottawa, Ontario: University of Ottawa.

Nagy, W.E., Herman, P.A., & Anderson, R.C. (1985). Learning words from context. *Reading Research Quarterly, 20*, 233–253.

Ng, S.M. (1987). *Annual report on the reading and English acquisition programme*. Singapore: Ministry of Education.

Schon, I., Hopkins, K.D., & Davis, W.A. (1982). The effects of books in Spanish and free reading time on Hispanic students' reading abilities and attitudes. *National Association of Bilingual Education Journal, 7*, 13–20.

9 | Donated Book Programs: An Interim Measure

*Rosamaria Durand
and Suzanne M. Deehy*

WHEN DEVELOPING COUNTRIES are unable to satisfy the demand for educational and reading materials on their own through local production or purchase, book donation programs from industrialized countries often serve as an interim measure. Donation agencies provide gifts of books as a temporary solution until an adequate book market and industry is established.

Are the donated books really gifts from overseas, or do they do more harm than good? In many cases, donated book programs have been regarded as peripheral to international development efforts, and perceptions of these particular efforts often have been quite negative. Concerns about donated book programs, mentioned in earlier chapters, have been grounded in the notion that these programs threaten the existence and the growth of local publishing industries and contribute only marginally to the development of reading materials. However, many donors and recipients of books believe that the contributions are doing more good than harm.

The goal of most successful donation programs is to provide the necessary educational materials for classroom instruction and outside reading to help improve literacy and learning, without disrupting existing or nascent local publishing efforts. Closely monitored and sensitively administered programs can achieve this goal and help develop better reading habits among students. In turn, this effort will support

local publishing industries in the future. Programs that are demand driven, rather than donor driven, have been the most successful in attaining their and the recipient country's goals. This chapter will demonstrate how donors and recipients can work together to make a valuable
contribution to reading through responsible donation schemes.

Book Needs and the Efforts to Satisfy Them

The widespread shortage of appropriate reading and instructional
materials in developing countries (United Nations Educational, Scientific and Cultural Organization, 1992) and the effect that this shortage
has on the development of education and specifically reading achievements is well known. Studies (Guthrie & Greaney, 1991; World Bank,
1988) repeatedly point to the availability of reading and instructional
materials as keys to promoting educational achievement, as mentioned
throughout this volume. The lack of educational materials in developing countries is attributed to a number of economic, technical, institutional, and legal factors. The severe undersupply of materials in developing countries, coupled with the lack of a local publishing industry,
has resulted in entire generations of young people having little or no
access to books.

This paucity of reading materials in developing countries is in
extreme contrast to the large surplus of books in industrialized countries. In the United States alone about 40 million new books are destroyed each year. Reasons for destruction vary from overproduction to
tax considerations to high storage costs. Although only a small portion
of the destroyed books are appropriate for donation, invaluable contributions can be made to education and the development of reading
habits through a program that carefully selects and places these
books. Western book donation agencies are working with counterparts
in many developing countries to match the appropriate surplus materials available from industrialized countries with the needs in the recipient countries.

Donated books are provided by myriad agencies. Among on-going
donation programs, some agencies specialize in university-level materials, others in elementary textbooks, and others focus on non-

school-related reading and library materials. In the United States and Canada, there are several major book donation agencies that provide large quantities of books to many different countries. Dozens of smaller civic, community, religious, and private voluntary organizations also donate books to particular countries; this is done usually on a small scale as a sideline to other activities. Western European and Australian donation schemes also provide much needed materials, although the agencies in these countries are smaller and fewer than those in the United States, where tax incentives encourage donation. Together each year the agencies dispatch millions of books to developing countries. A comprehensive list of book donors can be found in *Donated Book Programs: A Dialogue of Partners Handbook*, prepared by the International Book Bank and published by the Library of Congress in 1993.

The donated books themselves come from various sources including commercial publishers, nonprofit presses, school systems, bookstores, libraries, and individuals. Those books most often available for donation are secondary- and postsecondary-level textbooks from commercial publishers. Because new editions of these books are constantly being printed in developed countries, earlier editions are considered obsolete in the marketplace. The main beneficiaries tend to be universities and libraries, which keep the books in their holdings as supplemental materials. School systems represent another large source of donated books; they tend to buy new books and donate the old texts and readers to donation agencies. These books are sent to elementary schools and public libraries abroad to help promote reading and learning. In many cases, these books do not replace primary instructional texts prescribed by local government ministries; instead, the books are used as ancillary materials and provide teachers and students with additional sources of reading and information.

The largest percentage of donated books comes from the United States. This can be attributed to the size of the U.S. publishing industry, the number of books available, and a provision in U.S. tax regulations that allows an enhanced deduction for commercial publishers who donate books from their active inventories to qualified charitable organizations serving the needy, the ill, or children. At least 2 to 4 million books are donated each year under this tax rubric. Millions more books are available from the other sources mentioned earlier and from publishers who donate from their backlists.

Limitations of Book Donation Programs

On December 23, 1989, a devastating fire raged through the halls of the Central University Library in Bucharest, Romania, destroying much of the library's holdings and leaving an enormous void in the cultural and educational life of the country. In the wake of this tragic event, the international community responded rapidly and with generous intentions to a plea for help from the library. Individuals and organizations in many countries collected large numbers of books and journals and shipped them to Bucharest. Unfortunately, many of the goodwill gestures did not meet the needs of the library or make up for the losses of the tragic fire. Although some of the donated materials proved to be useful, a large percentage was inappropriate and outdated.

At the 1992 Dialogue of Partners conference—an international meeting of donor agencies, distribution agencies, and recipients—a delegate from the Central University Library in Romania remarked, "Unfortunately, some donations seem to have been sent over out of a charity feeling only, having no relevance, in respect to their content, to Romanian readers. These publications were useless because they referred to non-Romanian, irrelevant topics such as weather reports for foreign airports...old telephone books..." (*Donated Book Programs: A Dialogue of Partners Handbook*, International Book Bank, 1993, p. 36). The delegates stressed the importance for recipient organizations to be specific about their needs and not afraid to reject inappropriate donations. The Romanian example highlights the need for donors to sort donations before shipment.

Donations schemes such as a shipment of books written in Arabic to Uganda, where no one reads Arabic, and of manuals on filing U.S. tax returns to Kenya have undermined the donor-recipient partnership. By sending unwanted materials, some donors have clogged distribution systems, appropriated scarce library shelf space, consumed meager resources, and created a sense of distrust among recipient organizations.

These examples of harmful and irresponsible donations are neither isolated nor unique. Other schemes have included sending to developing countries study guides without texts, outdated travel guides, thousands of copies of obscure titles for which there was minimal need, indices for missing reference materials, and outdated computer manuals. Known in the professional jargon of practitioners as "dumping," the practice of sending materials such as these has been undertaken by ad-hoc donation programs and other donors who believe that "any book is better than no book at all." These types of inappropriate donated materials do little to encourage reading and have reinforced a negative perception that donated book programs are, at best, marginal to development.

Dumping happens far less often than responsible donating, even though the earlier examples of the practice are frequently cited by critics of the programs. The more established programs strive to ensure that donated book programs cease to be regarded as charity efforts and that they play a constructive role in the international development arena.

Responsible Partnerships

Within the existing limitations inherent to book donation programs, responsible and sensitive donors working together can make invaluable contributions to the development of education and reading habits. An appropriate book that responds to the expressed needs of a recipient is a useful gift—an instrument of development and a tool that promotes better reading habits.

The recipients must take an increasingly proactive role in the implementation of donated book programs. There is a symbiotic relationship between donor and recipients, and together they must strive toward the development of a mutually supportive rapport. This cooperation should result in

- donors gaining a greater understanding of the recipients' needs and soliciting and procuring materials that match these needs;
- recipients acquiring an accurate understanding of the types of materials that can be procured through donation programs;
- both sides securing resources to support the development of local distribution mechanisms; and
- both donors and recipients striving to professionalize and legitimize donated book programs.

Appropriate reading material provided by a donor program that responds to the expressed needs of a recipient is a useful gift—a gift that promotes better reading habits. © Jackie Garvey.

Although the 1992 Dialogue of Partners conference (International Book Bank, 1993) made progress in fostering increasingly productive and mutually supportive relationships between book donors and recipients, much more communication and collaboration need to occur, and the recipient needs to be more involved in the entire donation process.

Successful Donated Book Programs

Donated book programs cannot exist in isolation. To be successful, the donors must work with recipients to acquire an in-depth and specific knowledge of the country in which they wish to operate. Programs must be well targeted and donors must be cognizant of specific linguistic, cultural, and educational conditions.

In particular, programs must be supportive of, or at least not undermine, local publishing endeavors. Some donors have chosen to focus their efforts in the area of secondary- and postsecondary-level materials so they do not compete with the growing market of locally produced primary-level materials in many developing countries. As local publishers in developing countries recognize the lack of a viable reading market as a major constraint to their development, some are beginning to understand and accept the role that donated book programs can play in their countries. A delegate from the African Publishers' Network at the Dialogue of Partners conference noted that her organization views book donations as part of the long-term development of an indigenous publishing capacity, and it accepts the use of book donations both to complement the existing publishing industries and to fulfill the urgent necessities in book supply. At least one organization, the Canadian Organization for Development through Education, works in cooperation with local publishing industries in Africa, providing technical and material support. Because donated book programs neither provide a steady supply of books nor assure that multiple copies of the same title will be donated, they should not be viewed as a substitute for a local publishing industry.

Responsible donors develop partnerships with recipient organizations and work to identify book needs and establish procedures to best meet those needs. Some donors establish procedures in which the book selection is done by the donor, using specific information and guidelines from recipient libraries; other donors allow the recipient organizations to select materials either from booklists, book samples, or in person from the donor's warehouse.

Book Aid International in the United Kingdom, which ships approximately 700,000 books per year directly to libraries in developing countries, employs qualified librarians to select materials in direct response to library requests. The International Book Bank (IBB) and Sabre Foundation in the United States send shipments totaling more than 2 million books per year to partner organizations for redistribution to libraries. Both follow the booklist system: they offer books by title and quantity in response to requests by the distributing organization. Using the bibliographic information (with annotations in the case of IBB), the distributing organization can act like a customer and determine appropriate titles and quantities for distribution to local libraries. All approaches taken by successful programs give consideration to the specified needs in the recipient countries and involve communication between the donors and recipients. Where there are no financial limitations, the books should be reviewed either at the warehouse or prior to distribution through the provision of sample copies. Because of the differences in size, scope, and geographical involvement among donated book programs, it is difficult to make definitive prescriptions for the effective and efficient management of these programs. Lessons learned to date from major book donation agencies underline the importance of the following two basic principles:

1. "Know thy recipient." This is the guiding principle for a successful book donation program. It implies that the donor should not only understand and respond to expressed local needs, but also recognize the level of commitment, motivation, and political will that is likely to influence the partnership between the donors and recipients.

2. Book donation programs should be demand driven. The importance of the recipients' involvement in the selection process cannot be overemphasized. Methodologies can vary from providing recipients with lists of titles, annotated booklists, or actual book samples.

In addition, many donor agencies set internal guidelines for accepting donated books based on such factors as physical quality, date of publication (a cut-off year may be critical for scientific and technical materials), content, language appropriateness, and completeness (all ancillary materials should be accompanied by a text). When the donor agencies have discarded all the inappropriate materials, the selection process by the recipient becomes significantly easier.

Delivery of Donated Books

Methods of delivery of donated books vary from sending packages through the mail to shipping full containers of books on cargo ships. The delivery method chosen by the donation agency depends on its capacity for storage and loading, funding available to the agency for shipping, quantity of appropriate books for a particular destination, and the storage capacity of the recipient. The type of recipient also may determine the method of shipping: if the recipient is also a distributor of books to other schools and libraries, then a large volume of books might be sent; if the recipient is the end-user, a smaller shipment may suffice.

The most cost-effective method of transporting books is via ocean freight in sea containers, which typically hold between 15,000 and 25,000 volumes. Containerized shipments are consigned directly to the recipient, minimizing the danger of damage or theft. Book donation agencies have estimated that the per-book cost of containerized shipping varies, depending on the final destination. In most cases, the donating agency covers the costs of shipping from various funding sources, which include government grants, private foundation and corporate grants, and contributions from individuals and community organizations

Less than container load (LCL) and break bulk (BB) shipping via ocean freight are alternatives to containerized shipping when the quantity of books is too small for a container and too large to be mailed. In an LCL shipment, palletized books share container space with other goods and may be moved from one container to another before arriving at the final destination. In BB shipping, books are not packed in containers and can be stored anywhere on the ship, including the deck, in strapped and shrink-wrapped, secured pallets. However, LCL and BB shipping have drawbacks because the books are more susceptible to theft and physical damage. The per-unit costs are also greater than with containerized shipping.

Small quantities of books can be sent by surface mail, air mail, or in mail bags. Mail bags are canvas postal bags for shipping boxed printed material (up to a certain weight) to a particular destination abroad. It is nonpriority mail and travels by surface. This method is used by many smaller donation agencies and library exchange programs. It is more expensive than containerized shipping, and books cannot be insured or traced in case of loss.

In addition to shipping costs, a book donor also incurs processing, storage, and administrative charges. These vary significantly among donation agencies, depending on the volume of books shipped, the level of screening and selection, the level of technology used, and amount of information provided to recipients for selection.

Once book shipments arrive in their country of destination, the recipient organization takes responsibility for placement in schools and libraries, although some recipients are the end-users. In the United States, suitability of recipients must be determined in accordance with Internal Revenue Service guidelines, if donated materials are received in accordance with the terms of the tax-deduction ruling, as mentioned earlier. Under this ruling, the consignee must be a nongovernmental, nonprofit equivalent organization. The donated books can then be distributed by the consignee to government-run schools and libraries, which act as "holding institutions" by holding the books in trust for those who need them.

Evaluation of Donated Book Programs

As with any development program, periodic evaluations and monitoring are a necessary part of the process and are useful for both donor and recipient. Questionnaires and on-site evaluations are most commonly used. Questionnaires are typically sent by donor agencies to recipient organizations following a book shipment. They cover such topics as appropriateness and usefulness of materials; physical condition of the shipment upon arrival; accuracy of the packing list; shipment and customs details; warehousing and distribution issues; and suggestions to the donor regarding titles, selection, packaging, and labeling. On-site evaluations, performed by either the agencies or qualified personnel, focus on the end-user libraries. They provide the donor with such information as where, how, and by whom the donated books are being used. In addition, on-site visits give the donor agency the opportunity to explore broader issues including the program's effect on reading habits and education; the plight of the local publishing industry; the impact of donated books on that industry; other book donation activities; and political, economic, or legal changes that may affect future donations.

Conducted properly, evaluations provide valuable feedback to all involved in the book donation process, from the donating publishers to the donor agencies and the recipients. The evaluation results, both positive and negative, can be used to improve the overall process of book donation and to meet the specific—and changing—needs in each country. Responsibility for conducting a useful evaluation belongs to the donor agency and the recipient organization, and it must be an integral part of the book donation process.

Final Comments

Provided they are consistent with the book development strategy of a country and in agreement with local publishers and recipients, donated book programs can and do have a significant educational impact, specifically on the development of a reading culture and the local book industry. To meet their objectives, donated book programs must be responsibly managed and have adequate human, financial, and in-kind resources.

Ultimately, the success of these endeavors depends on major donor agencies' understanding that donated book programs have a role in international development. They can assist by helping create an adequate infrastructure for the responsible processing and distribution of donated materials.

Donated book programs respond to immediate needs and represent a short-term solution for providing an adequate supply of appropriate reading materials. The long-term solution is a viable indigenous publishing industry.

References

Guthrie, J.T., & Greaney, V. (1991). Literacy acts. In R. Barr, M.L. Kamil, P. Mosenthal, & P.D. Pearson (Eds.), *Handbook of reading research: Volume II* (pp. 68–96). White Plains, NY: Longman.

International Book Bank. (1993). *Donated book programs: A Dialogue of Partners handbook*. Washington, DC: Library of Congress.

United Nations Educational, Scientific and Cultural Organization. (1992). *Statistical Yearbook*, 1992. Paris: Author.

World Bank. (1988). *Education in Sub-Saharan Africa: Policies for adjustment, revitalization, and expansion*. Washington, DC: Author.

10 | Libraries and Literacy in Developing Countries

Rebecca Knuth, Barbara Perry, and Brigitte Duces

TOO OFTEN LITERACY efforts in developing countries have been conceptualized as a product-oriented process in which adults pass simple tests and literacy figures improve. This linear thinking ignores the systemic quality of literacy, the necessity for supporting structures, literacy's role in personal and societal development, and the need for a reason to read in daily life—in essence, the role of literacy in both creating and being sustained by a literate environment. Linear thinking ignores the reality of literacy development as a two-phase process: first, successful guided instruction leads to acquisition of reading skills; second, use and maintenance of acquired skills are practiced through reading a variety of materials. It ignores the need to integrate formal and nonformal education efforts and to shift from thinking about literacy solely as an individual endeavor to appreciating literacy acquisition as a community, familial, and societal enterprise.

As mentioned earlier in this volume, literacy campaigns in developing countries frequently result in a surge of new literates who have little to read. Formal education often fails to achieve its goal as many children leave school prematurely before mastering basic reading skills, whereas some other children face a world where their reading skills are irrelevant and unsustainable. Intense pressure on teachers to prepare students for standardized examinations (Dore, 1976; Kellaghan & Greaney, 1992) results in many students memorizing large tracts of textbooks without ever developing higher order comprehension skills or a liking for reading. Unfortunately, government programs tend to stress the technical skills of reading and writing, while failing to devote sufficient attention to the importance of knowledge and access to knowledge for the rural poor and those who leave school prematurely (Semali, 1991).

Literacy support initiatives tend to yield results when literacy is approached systemically and when significant attention is paid to support structures such as publishing houses, generation of indigenous reading materials, government advocacy of formal and informal reading programs, reading as a habit, and provision of libraries. This latter element, library provision in developing countries, is the focus of this chapter.

Library Support of Literacy in Developing Countries

Traditional libraries in developed countries are often not suited to local conditions in developing countries, especially in rural areas. Western library models have developed over time and through adaptive processes in support of gradually industrializing, literate, and eventually information-based societies. Libraries were established on the assumption that a "reading population" existed. Book collections were targeted to the literate. Various delivery systems were tried, and certain institutional structures evolved and gained acceptance.

In developed countries, libraries have helped meet the recreational and informational needs of the middle class. The connection between libraries and literacy is implicit. Libraries have become an aspect of literate society that is usually taken for granted.

In developing countries, precolonial libraries were urban based and existed for the elite (Mabomba, 1993). Public libraries that have been established in independent countries frequently continue to serve the elite or function as reading rooms for examination-bound students, many of whom use their own books (Akinnigbagbe, 1982). Libraries have failed to meet the needs of the majority—children, the poor, rural populations, and neoliterates. In most cities, scarcity of resources has resulted in outdated, haphazard collections, often supplemented by donations and discards of dubious value. Mchombu

(1993) reported, "The amount of usable information reaching rural areas is still dismally low" (p. 9). It is recognized that the need in rural communities for information for development is growing. However, libraries lack a vision of an appropriate service-oriented mission for developing societies. Rather than serve as traditional, passive institutions staffed by caretakers of materials, libraries must be reconceptualized as people-oriented services that serve as informational, cultural, and educational centers (Korten, 1984).

Alternative Models to Traditional Libraries

In developing countries, explicit linkages between libraries and information users can be forged by the evolution of alternative models to traditional public libraries. Some examples are explained in the following sections.

In developing countries, library provision—particularly alternative models to traditional public libraries—should be a priority. ©Pamela Winsor. Used by permission.

Mobile Libraries

Mobile libraries bring books to people by various forms of transport including cars, vans, boats, river rafts, bicycles, motorcycles, carts, and wagons. Innovations include "book boxes," such as those developed for Thailand's Portable Library project: boxes were moved from place to place and unfolded to become free-standing bookshelves lined with books (Stan, 1990). Slings have been devised so that hammocks holding books may be hung from trees. In Asia, "barefoot librarians" carry packets of books on their backs. Even in times of war, mobile libraries have provided books to those in need. In Beirut during the civil strife, books were taken on carts to old movie theaters and other shelters housing homeless families (Stan, 1990). In the highlands of Peru, newspapers and health pamphlets formed the basis of a traveling library: "Literates would read aloud to the uneducated, engendering an unprecedented awareness of the world beyond the Altiplano" (Hazen, 1981, p. 410). In Papua New Guinea, "developmental information workers" traveled from village to village showing videos to facilitate dialogue on development issues (Ahai, 1990).

Drawbacks to mobile library schemes include the lack of consistent provision of transportation resources. Fiji's interisland book bag scheme began in 1970 but lapsed in 1986 due to land and sea transportation problems (International Association of School Librarianship, 1993). Other impediments include a lack of personnel to accompany books and limitations on collections that must be frequently changed or renewed.

Some organizations have helped foster the idea of mobile libraries as well. The United Nations Educational, Scientific and Cultural Organization (UNESCO) and the Children's Reading Development Association at Bangkok's Sri Nakharinwirot University organized a traveling exhibition for young readers in 1989 and 1990. The exhibition aimed to open the world of books to children and make them aware of subjects such as peace; human rights; literacy; the environment; drug abuse; and cultural, economic, and social development. As part of the exhibition, workshops familiarized teachers and librarians with methods and techniques to attract young people to books. Replica book sets were deposited in regional libraries.

Rotating Collections

Rotating collections are books that are rotated among schools, public libraries, or other suitable locations. Rotating collections may be part of larger programs in which public libraries link with local literacy programs. For example, adult literacy classes may be held in libraries that have rotating collections. Using rotating collections is often the method of choice for school library services in areas unable to sustain viable individual collections within schools. In addition, rotating collections among schools is often a first step in development of effective school libraries. Drawbacks include the difficulties of transporting materials, security of materials, and maintaining enough funds for the rotation.

Village Reading Corners

Establishing small collections of books accessible to users in rural areas and villages is a regular feature of postliteracy programs. Success lies in designing collections that are appropriate to the needs and interests of users. Problems with the model are apparent when village collections consist of well-intentioned but misguided book choices that are too difficult, too literary, or on subjects of no interest to the average villager or child. Unattended centers may also be less effective because new literates benefit from the support of an intermediary or guide to reading (Richardson, 1983).

In Africa, rural community information centers, where small collections of books are held, were established widely during the 1980s. Although intended to be used by the entire community and to be staffed and operated by community volunteers, they are used primarily by school children (Priestley, 1995). It is not clear what the impact of these centers has been and how this type of service should be evaluated and assessed.

Use of Nonprint Media and Extra-Library Activities

The concept of library collections has expanded to include use of audiotapes, television, videotapes, pictures, posters, and other media resources to supplement the written word. Audiovisual materials offer an advantage through their appeal to various modes of learning.

Unfortunately, in many instances these materials cannot be used because of power failures (Akinnigbagbe, 1982).

In community-based approaches, such as Mali's Operation Lecture Publique, rural libraries promote reading with children and their families and organize extensive book-related activities including storytelling, plays, games, and taping of local traditional oral materials (International Association of School Librarianship, 1992). Village elders have been invited to libraries to serve as traditional information sources. Indigenous images have been generated by local people and silk-screened into "shell books"—books that tell a story through pictures; text in various indigenous languages is then added (Ahai, 1991).

Innovative library-based programs help introduce largely oral cultures to the world of print, and media assist in the integration of the library into the larger culture and community. Rather than acting as simply repositories of materials, libraries can serve as instructional centers on health, literacy, and childcare (Onadiran & Onadiran, 1984) or as community centers that feature referral and counseling services, exhibitions, literacy competitions, demonstrations, and cultural performances.

Innovative extra-library options include home libraries such as those in Zimbabwe. Begun as a project to expose children to short stories in their indigenous language, these libraries evolved into small home collections for neighborhood children, kept by mothers who read aloud to their children and others (Patte & Geradts, 1985). Goals include introducing children to the concept of reading for pleasure, using the home library process as a link between generations, motivating parents, and encouraging new literates to use their gained literacy skills for reading aloud simple stories in their own languages (Waungana, 1990).

Modern School Libraries

In some countries, increased attention is being directed to a model that combines the school and public library facilities. This model supplies a framework in which libraries can serve all the people by contributing to a literate environment and literacy efforts, while supporting formal education and development programs (Knuth, 1994). There is also a trend to provide reading rooms that are linked to formal and informal educational structures. In Ethiopia, a plan advocates creation of common schools or reading areas in which both adult and child are educated. This shows particular promise because it unites families and the community in learning while making multiple uses of scarce resources. The Colombian model of the school library providing material and support for the adult village community, described in Chapter 6, is a further example of this important linkage.

Programs in Various Developing Countries

Approaches to supporting literacy with library services take different forms in different countries. Lessons learned from individual countries may help to design frameworks for the evolution of appropriate services for other developing countries.

Tanzania

The mass adult literacy program undertaken by Tanzania is one of the most extensively studied national literacy projects in the developing world. Initial work began in the late 1960s through Tanzania's participation in the Work-Oriented Adult Literacy Pilot Project (WOALP) sponsored by the United Nations Development Program (UNDP) and UNESCO. Since 1970, when the ambitious and extensive national program officially began, Tanzania's literacy work has been scrutinized by the Tanzanians and by the world education community. Initial and long-term program successes have been shown as an example for future international efforts. However, the current state of the program is also illustrative of difficulties that can beset literacy activities; the problems of the library components of the program outlined in the following fully reflect its course.

Conditions in rural life, such as dominance of oral communication, static environment, lack of readily accessible reading materials, lack of electricity and privacy, and huge distances to literacy classes greatly hinder the possibility of creating literate rural communities (Baregu, 1972). Planners of the Tanzanian literacy campaign attempted to address infrastructural problems by creating the Ujamaa villages (the Tanzanian model commune). Despite arguments that library structures should not be established before people are literate to use them, it was decided that people seeking literacy should be exposed to services even before they could read; materials should be available as they learned. The Tanzanian program advocated that literacy teachers could help students become aware of the potential of a library and teach book skills. By being established in the operational phase of a literacy program, the libraries could have more of an impact at the follow-up stage and assist in the formation of a literate environment (Baregu, 1972).

During the WOALP program, from 1968 to 1972, 90 rural libraries were established. Specialist groups including librarians formed to support the program. These groups produced initial adult literacy program materials that would later become part of core rural library collections. In addition to rural libraries, other literacy support elements that were established included rural newspapers, folk development colleges, and correspondence courses.

An initial goal of creating 2,000 rural libraries was set and further increased to 8,000   one for each village in the country. Each library was to have a core collection of 400 to 500 books in Swahili, the national language and language of literacy instruction. Books were provided to village libraries at no cost. Materials were geared to neoliterates and also served as reading materials for active readers. In addition, locally produced rural newspapers with a content suitable for neoliterates were available in each library. Village libraries were planned to house discussion groups and offer audiovisual presentations relevant to village activities, which would allow the library to become a village focal point for adult education. Villages were expected to construct simple structures to house their libraries. By 1985, approximately 3,000 libraries with a total collection in excess of 1 million volumes existed.

At the village level, individuals were selected by village leadership to coordinate access to materials. At the local level, rural librarians (often literacy teachers) were appointed after participating in a two-week course in library science. At the district level, district (or ward) librarians were selected from among ward adult education coordinators. During the 1980s, the staff of village and rural libraries numbered more than 3,400, most of whom were volunteers.

While the library component in the Tanzanian program continued to develop during the early 1980s, funding for collections largely evaporated. No new books were added to village libraries, and other literacy support programs struggled or were not undertaken. A service to refresh the village collection through regular exchange of materials had limited success due to poor transportation and insufficient titles. The mobile libraries program was discontinued because of equipment maintenance difficulties, high cost of fuel, and poor quality of roads. Construction of standardized buildings in villages to house libraries, establishment of discussion groups and community information centers, and appointment of professionally trained librarians did not take place.

As conceived, the Tanzanian literacy program was a comprehensive model for library support of postliteracy activities. Early progress has been eroded by a lack of funds, national economic uncertainty, and diminished government advocacy of literacy efforts.

Thailand

Literacy programs in Thailand can be traced to the 1940s when the first mass compulsory education campaign was launched. The most recent national literacy campaign developed from the government's document *Fifth National Economic and Social Development Plan* (1982–1985), in which clear targets for literacy education were set. Key concepts in this national campaign included voluntary participation, use of family and community literates as instructors, and decentralized program planning and administration. The administrative structure of the campaign was based on shared responsibilities. At the national level, the Thai Ministry of Education and the Departments of General Education and Nonformal Education were involved. Provincial authorities set targets for minimum literacy levels and worked with provincial education officers, chiefs of provincial nonformal education centers, and district education officers. Village leaders and committees oversaw village literacy activities.

The concept of the village reading center (VRC) has become a cornerstone for Thailand's literacy activities. Begun in 1972, VRCs were established as community resource centers built and operated by village committees. From 1983 to 1987 these centers increased in number from 8,100 to 28,000. By 1991, more than 30,000 VRCs existed. If the goal of establishing one VRC per village is attained, it will eventually result in 68,000 centers. Government support includes materials for new literates produced by the ministries of agriculture, health, and education and funds to purchase newspapers and enhance book collections. VRCs coordinate with other literacy activities including mobile libraries and rotating collections. It is estimated that there are on average 15 to 18 users of individual VRCs daily and that 60% of literacy graduates use them regularly (Limtrakarn, 1990).

A review of the program (Suntornpithug, 1986) indicates that the massive increase in the number of VRCs during the 1980s has resulted in considerable variation in quality of and commitment to the program throughout the country. The success of a given VRC can be directly linked to the community support provided to it through the village committee. A central village location also contributes to the level of usage of VRCs. Among other results of the review are indications that book collections need to be evaluated in terms of their relevance to literacy programs and readers, newspapers are not always current, VRC caretakers need training, and facilities need to be improved.

In addition to VRCs, other literacy initiatives in Thailand include the provision of temple reading centers (more than 2,300), in Buddhist temples; public libraries in both urban and rural areas, including 70 provincial libraries and 315 district libraries that organize book rotation schemes to villages and mobile services; radio programs promoting reading; library linkages to correspondence courses and open university programs; print materials from regional nonformal education centers; and community information services sponsored by the Thai Library Association linking existing community, school, and other local resources.

Jamaica

Jamaica has approached the problem of sustainability of literacy skills by formally linking public library services with local literacy programs. In the 1970s, and to a lesser degree since then, the Jamaica Library Service (JLS) worked closely with the Jamaican Movement for the Advancement of Literacy (JAMAL) to support literacy programs. Established in 1974, JAMAL's goals include eradication of illiteracy, improvement of literacy skills, and development of human resources. Achievement of these goals was hampered by the lack of ready access by new literates to interesting and simple reading materials.

The Jamaican Library Service provided new literates reading material through 55 parish and branch libraries and 143 bookmobile stops (Jamaican Movement for the Advancement of Literacy Foundation, 1981). Its efforts included generation of booklists, literacy competitions, a "New Readers" page in Jamaica's largest newspaper, production of a monthly newspaper called "Let's Read," and encouragement of local writers. JLS's book selection policy emphasized diversity in nonfiction materials, variety rather than duplication in fiction selections, and a balance between serious and popular works and materials for new literates. Outreach programs included bookmobiles at JAMAL graduation ceremonies to register new graduates and introduce them to JLS services; purchase of large-print books and special collections with easy materials; book exhibitions, booklists for new literates, and educational tours of libraries; use of library buildings for JAMAL teacher training, advanced classes, and other activities; and follow-up advice and motivational activities for new literates by the JAMAL Graduate Library Appreciation Programme.

In the area of human resource development, both JLS and JAMAL sponsored lectures, training courses, seminars, and workshops in book production and writing for new literates. With the support of UNESCO and UNDP, Project Fulfil was launched to provide follow-up reading material for new literates. The aim was to "foster work of a popular nature such as short stories, novels, plays, and comic strips based on themes of West Indian folk life, biography, travel and adventures, and stories of religious inspiration. Accent was placed on reading for pleasure so as to inculcate the reading habit to improve the quality of life of new literates" (Jamaican Movement for the Advancement of Literacy Foundation, 1981, p. 239).

The partnership between JAMAL and JLS deteriorated somewhat in the late 1980s. Funding was an overriding problem in both organizations. JLS was not able to provide as much support as in earlier years. JAMAL had difficulty carrying out its activities because of widespread social program cuts and reductions in staff. JAMAL support has been transferred from the national literacy campaign model to an emphasis on workplace literacy. According to a 1995 interview with Lascelles Lewis, Director of JAMAL, the shift has been prompted by the reduction in resources and by the results of surveys showing that literacy levels had risen (from 47% in 1975 to 75.8% in 1994) and that workforce productivity was low (L. Lewis, personal communication, March 1995).

Overall, JAMAL is shifting from a focus on basic literacy to the ability to use information skills for survival in daily life and on the job, numeracy skills, and adult education. It is joining forces with the national vocational training agency (Human Employment and Resources Training Trust) to develop skills for young trainees. Libraries have been chosen to play an important role in the new initiative.

Venezuela

In contrast to Jamaica's interagency cooperation, Venezuela provides an example of the efficacy of a private institution's influence on construction of literacy structures. Banco del Libro began in the early 1960s and has been characterized as "an institution of firsts" (Uribe, 1988, p. 5). It created the first public and school libraries in Venezuela in 1965 and launched the first children's book publishing program, Ediciones Ekaré, which strives to publish children's collections with an accent on tales, legends, and poems based on oral tradition. Collections include stories about real-life contemporary situations and indigenous groups and nonfiction books about Venezuela. Ediciones Ekaré has mass produced materials for rural populations for free distribution to schools or at low cost to the general population through nontraditional outlets.

With Organization of American States support, Banco del Libro formulated a model and prototype for a rural library, which was to improve the quality of the educational process, stimulate reading throughout the community, and support the development of teachers. This successful model involved a nongovernmental organization that rallied government support and established an extensive research component, as well as provided opportunities for wide reading in the community. Further details are given in Chapter 6.

Nigeria

Nigerians have traditionally been leaders in African librarianship, particularly in school librarianship. The Nigerian School Library Association has been active in the formulation of standards, manuals, and training opportunities. School libraries have been advocated in various national education policies. In addition, primary school libraries were included in the World Bank's Primary Education Project for Nigeria (Elaturoti, 1993).

The University of Ibadan's Abadina Media Resource Center (AMRC) functions as a center for research and as a model school library media center. The center experiments with programs that reduce negative effects on children from their socioeconomic and cultural environment, transmit knowledge and information on cultural heritage, and teach children to exploit the resources of the library as part of education (Ogunsheye, 1979). Serving as a multipurpose institution, the AMRC has become a social center for parents and seeks to involve them in their children's education.

According to two government officials, libraries in Nigeria do not support adult literacy programs, despite part of the National Policy of Education, which states that "government will encourage the greatly increased adult education programmes by library support services" (Aji & Moda, 1994, p. 11). Aji and Moda call for collaboration by federal and state governments; integration of the efforts of academic, school, and public librarians; and alliances with publishers, professional associations, and the National Book Development Council. They argue that librarians must become involved at all levels of education, work with various agencies, collaborate with the media and writers, establish core comprehensive materials collections, and work with literacy workers and the learners themselves. Librarians can serve as liaisons between literacy programs and the library or between students and teachers; they can also run literacy clubs and discussion groups. These ideas complement the work of Gassol de Horowitz (1993) of Venezuela, who promotes librarianship as a change agent in development processes in developing countries.

Malaysia

Malaysia is attempting a new cultural orientation toward literacy with government campaigns designed to create a thinking society. Literacy efforts are viewed as nation building, and reading is perceived as linked to the nation's social and economic progress. The development of the reading habit is to be fostered at all levels, and attention is to be given to creating the infrastructures of a literate society, through such initiatives as promotion of publishing, encouragement of authors, and adult literacy programs (Knuth, 1993).

After independence, in 1963 the Malaysian government assumed responsibility for creation of a literate environment. By directing reading promotion efforts toward the children, who make up 40% of the population, the government hoped to transform reading habits of the nation as a whole. This meant dealing with various problems that prevented or impeded development of the reading habit throughout Asia. These problems include illiteracy or marginal literacy, high primary school dropout rates, scarcity of inexpensive books in national languages, lack of rural bookstores, home and school environments that do not encourage reading, and lack of libraries (Anuar, 1985).

To compensate for environments that do not support reading, the Malaysian government concentrated on building new schools and improving existing educational programs. Substantial investment was made in reading initiatives and in establishing book collections in the schools. The National Language and Literature Development Agency (Dewan Bahasa dan Pustaka, DBP) was established to handle problems of book production and lack of local language materials (Rustam, 1990). Other problems to be addressed included small print runs and lack of incentives for authors and publishers, resulting in a lack of interesting indigenous materials. The DBP solved difficulties of book distribution by setting up book distributors and regional marketing centers.

Earlier studies of Malaysian public libraries revealed a significant pattern of underutilization because Malaysians did not consider the library a major source of reading materials (Lim, 1986). This problem was approached directly by improvement of book collections and indirectly by efforts to encourage the reading habit. School libraries were improved and extended so that children would experience libraries as part of their educational experience. Teachers were trained to avoid an overdependence on textbooks and to expose children to books within the educational context. Teachers were expected to encourage reading by their students as a way to compensate for literacy-impoverished home environments.

Gradually, school librarians were introduced into the schools to provide extensive reading guidance, motivational activities, and resources. To encourage an approach that reaches beyond literacy development to information use, dependence on rote learning and textbook teaching was deemphasized. Children should be taught to find, use, and interpret information and extend their ability to think critically (Yaacob & Seman, 1993).

Multilateral and Nongovernmental Organization Involvement

Organizations such as UNESCO and the International Federation of Library Associations and Institutions (IFLA) have supported the work of local librarians or government officials in many ways. "Key Policy Issues in International Book, Library, and Information Development" was the theme of an international conference jointly sponsored by International Book Development and IFLA. Other associations such as the International Association of School Librarianship and the International Board on Books for Young People have issued awards, seed money, and leadership grants; provided seminars and workshops; and served as informational forums. However, because of budgetary, communication, and networking limitations and the worldwide scope of efforts, there has been scattering of energy and a relative lack of visibility of library services in literacy programs.

International symposia and conferences on literacy tend to ignore the role of libraries in discussions on adult or functional literacy efforts. For instance, the discussion documents from the World Conference on Education for All in Thailand in March 1990 (sponsored by UNICEF, UNDP, and the World Bank) did not mention libraries. However, the presence of the president of the International Association for School Librarianship was instrumental in winning acceptance of the role of libraries as partners in education through inclusion of an endorsement concerning libraries in the final documents (Thomas, 1990).

Multilateral and nongovernmental organizations are ill served by the quality of data available on libraries in individual countries. For instance, the UNESCO Statistical Yearbook (1994) lists a single library in Thailand (the national library), although library-type services, as indicated earlier, are widespread. This is an area in which further effort of the international library community might be focused.

Changing Our Thinking About Libraries and Literacy for the Future

Programs and models discussed in this chapter indicate that effective library-supported literacy programs tend to be integrated with wider systems within the community or nation. At the local level, successful libraries or information centers are explicitly unified with community activities and literacy programs. Sustainable local efforts rely on regionwide support systems that provide transportation of materials, training for personnel, and expansion of collections. For this support, regional systems need a strong commitment from senior officials in government. Good campaign plans take into account not only the immediate goals of making people literate but also long-term plans for maintaining literacy after basic skills are acquired. This need for sustainability requires a network of institutions, all working together with strong commitment to deliver services. The network includes national government ministries, the publishing industry including the book distribution trade, and local government officials. A library system should be one element within this overall network.

For too long, traditional library models have served to limit thinking and delivery of services and marginalize the role of libraries in literacy efforts. Public, school, and community libraries must be understood as part of one integrated system. Implementation designs need to be based on literacy, community, and information needs, rather than on predetermined delivery models. At the national level, planners should think in terms of national information systems. At the local level, combined public and school libraries are receiving increased attention as a way of meeting the needs of all generations (Knuth, 1994). Boundaries between formal and informal education efforts are blurring in countries such as Ethiopia, where it is proposed that schools integrate formal and informal literacy efforts in one building. Worldwide, UNESCO leads a movement toward a reconceptualization of literacy support systems geared toward the family rather than the individual.

Paradigms for development have undergone constant change, most significantly from a focus on economic development to an appreciation of people-centered concerns. Concepts of literacy as being essential to economic development have become more important as concepts of the development of human resources have evolved to include acknowledgment of the right to learn as a priority (Watson, 1985). Literacy not only enables a population to have greater ability to use resources and participate in economic development, it also is justified as an innate human right. Literacy is increasingly discussed in systemic terms (Bhola, 1993) and as part of economic, social, and political development. Just as our concepts of development have undergone constant change and have become increasingly holistic or systemic, our thinking about libraries and literacy must evolve if we hope to welcome all people into a world of literacy.

References

Ahai, N. (1990). Literacy in an emergent society: Papua New Guinea. READ *Magazine*, 26, 3–13.

Aji, M.U., & Moda, M. (1994, March). *Public libraries and literacy campaigns: Objectives, roles and efforts made so far.* Paper presented at the National Consultative Forum of Chairmen of Library Boards in Akura, Nigeria.

Akinnigbagbe, B.M. (1982). Image of the public librarian in Nigeria: Need for a pragmatic change. *Libri*, 32, 156–162.

Anuar, H. (1985). The promotion of the reading habit. In H. Anuar (Ed.), *Issues in Southeast Asian librarianship* (pp. 83–194). Aldershot, England: Gower.

Baregu, M.L.M. (1972). Rural libraries in functional literacy campaigns. UNESCO *Bulletin for Libraries*, 26, 18–24.

Bhola, H.S. (1993). Systems thinking, literacy practice: Planning a literacy campaign in Egypt. In R. Packham (Ed.), *Ethical management of science as a system* (Proceedings of the 37th Annual Meeting of the International Society for the Systems Sciences, pp. 581–591). Sydney: University of Western Sydney.

Dore, R. (1976). *The diploma disease: Education, qualification, and development.* Berkeley, CA: University of California Press.

Elaturoti, D.F. (1993). Training school librarians for the Nigerian school system: A new perspective. In *Proceedings for the Annual Conference of the International Association for School Librarianship.* Kalamazoo, MI: International Association of School Librarianship.

Gassol de Horowitz, R. (1993). Literacy and development in the third world: Could librarianship make a difference? *International Federation of Library Associations and Institutions Journal*, 19, 170–180.

Hazen, D.C. (1981). Meanings of literacy in the third world: The concepts and consequences of the Rijchary reform movement in highland Peru. *Journal of Library History*, 16, 404–415.

International Association of School Librarianship. (1992). IBBY-ASAHI Reading Promotion Award. *International Association of School Librarianship Newsletter*, 21, 7.

International Association of School Librarianship. (1993). Book box scheme. *International Association of School Librarianship Newsletter*, 22, 12.

Jamaican Movement for the Advancement of Literacy Foundation. (1981). Literacy programmes and the public library service in Jamaica. UNESCO Journal, 3, 235–240.

Kellaghan, T., & Greaney, V. (1992). Using examinations to improve education (Technical Paper No. 165). Washington, DC: World Bank.

Knuth, R. (1993). Japan and Malaysia: How two countries promote the reading habit. International Review of Children's Literature and Librarianship, 8, 169–180.

Knuth, R. (1994). Libraries, literacy and development: Combined libraries as an option for developing countries: A brief communication. International Information and Library Review, 26, 77–89.

Korten, D. (1984). People-centered development: Toward a framework. In D. Korten & R. Klaus (Eds.), People-centered development: Contributions toward theory and planning frameworks. West Hartford, CT: Kumarian Press.

Lim, H. (1986). Public library services in Malaysia: An analysis. Library Review, 35, 5–12.

Limtrakarn, S. (1990). Literacy programmes in Thailand. Paper presented at the International Reading Association 13th World Congress on Reading, Stockholm, Sweden.

Mabomba, R.S. (1993). Improving access to information in Africa: The rural library service experiment in Malawi. Paper delivered at the International Federation of Library Associations and Institutions Conference, Barcelona, Spain.

Mchombu, K. (1993). A survey of information needs for rural development. Paper delivered at the International Federation of Library Associations and Institutions General Conference and Council Meeting, Barcelona, Spain.

Ogunsheye, F.A. (1979). Abadina Media Resource Center (AMRC): A case study in library service to primary schools. UNESCO Journal of Information Science, Librarianship and Archives Administration, 1, 29–36.

Onadiran, G., & Onadiran, R. (1984). Educational and informational needs of public library users in Nigeria. Public Library Quarterly, 5, 63–74.

Patte, G., & Geradts, A. (1985). Home libraries in Zimbabwe. IFLA Journal, 11, 223–227.

Priestley, C. (1995). Access to learning materials for pupils in Africa. London: International African Institute.

Richardson, J. (1983). Libraries and the neoliterate. International Library Review, 15, 9–13.

Rustam, R. (1990). Promoting literacy and reading in Malaysia: The role of Dewan Bahasa dan Pustaka. Information Development, 6, 440–459.

Semali, L.M. (1991). Postliteracy education in Tanzania and the retention of literacy skills in adults: The role of the communication media. Ph.D dissertation, University of California, Los Angeles.

Stan, S. (1990). IBBY Congress was uplifting—and in tune with times. Publisher's Weekly, 237, 38–39.

Suntornpithug, N. (1986). The development of learning strategies for post-literacy and continuing education of neoliterates in the perspective of lifelong education in Thailand. In Learning strategies for post-literacy and continuing education in China, India, Indonesia, Nepal, Thailand and Vietnam (UNESCO Institute for Education Studies on Post-Literacy and Continuing Education, No. 4). Hamburg,

Germany: United Nations Educational, Scientific and Cultural Organization, Institute for Education.

Thomas, L. (1990, July). Presidents' report. In *Proceedings of the Annual Conference of the International Association of School Librarianship*. Kalamazoo, MI: International Association of School Librarianship.

United Nations Educational, Scientific and Cultural Organization. (1994). *Statistical Yearbook*, 1994. Paris: Author.

Uribe, V. (1988). Banco del Libro of Venezuela: An institution of firsts. *Bookbird*, 26, 5–8.

Watson, G. (1985). The right to learn: A development priority. *Canadian Library Journal*, 42, 197–201.

Waungana, E. (1990). The Home Library Movement of Zimbabwe. *Bookbird*, 28, 18–19.

Yaacob, R.A., & Seman, N.A. (1993, September). Towards achieving a critical thinking society in Malaysia: A challenge to school libraries and educational systems. In *Proceedings of the Annual Conference of the International Association for School Librarianship* (pp. 10–23). Kalamazoo, MI: International Association of School Librarianship.

Author Index

Note: An "*f*" following an index entry indicates that the citation may be found in a figure, a "*t*" that it may be found in a table.

Subject Index

Note: An *"f"* following an index entry indicates that the citation may be found in a figure, a *"t"* that it may be found in a table.